Knitty Gritty

For the absolute beginner knitter

by Aneeta Patel

A&C Black ▪ London

photography by Peter Schiazza

First published in Great Britain in 2008

Reprinted in 2009, 2011

A & C Black Publishers Limited
36 Soho Square
London W1D 3QY

www.acblack.com

ISBN: 978-0-7136-85428

CIP Catalogue records for this book are available from
the British Library and the U.S. Library of Congress.

Cover design: Sutchinda Rangsi Thompson
Photography: Peter Schiazza
Commissioning Editor: Susan James

Printed and bound in China

This book is produced using paper that is made from
wood grown in managed, sustainable forests. It is
natural, renewable and recyclable. The logging
and manufacturing processes conform to the
environmental regulations of the country of origin.

Acknowledgments

Yarn and other knitting materials were kindly donated by the generous people at: Colinette, Debbie Bliss, Hipknits, I Knit London, Rowan and Sirdar. For contact details and more information, please see the Stockists list on page 124.

Thanks are due to my Guinea Pigs, the tireless beginner knitters who took up the challenge of testing the patterns in this book: Alison Steadman, Annabel Leathes, Annie Ng, Becky Clarke, Caroline Fonda, Catherine Alaguiry, Cathy Eatough, Charlie Kitchen, David O'Dwyer, David Vannen, Dawn Bray, Deborah Coughlin, Genevieve Grady, Guils Driver, Hannah Spencer, Hasu Patel, Hayley Dalton, Izzy Pugh, Jane Freimiller, Jayne Morgan, Jem Davis, Karen Eaton, Kate Ballinger, Kathie Schroeder, Libby Thomas, Marion Ohlson, Mary Cowin, Michelle Cain, Natalie Billington, Niki Stevens, Nutroast, Paula Ellis, Peter Brownell, Rachael Sutton, Sam Tyfield, Sarah Macleod, Seeta Patel, Sonja Petersen, Suresh Patel, Susan Neuville and Vicky Cowin. Without them I'd never have known where I was going wrong.

Thank you to all the models – born to wear knits: Adam Hilton, Alexander Whitamore, Alexis Larusson, Brie McAuley, Catherine Alaguiry, Charlie Kitchen, Daisy Beattie, Lilian Rose Wilson, Felix Ohlson, Harriet Morgan, Henry Schroeder, Isobel Morgan, Jake Stevens, Jayne Morgan, Jane Freimiller, Jem Davis, Jess Hilton, John Neuville, Jonathan Allen, Leah Bray, Lilia Larusson, Louis Strong, Lucy Neuville, Peter Brownell, Polly Adams, Rosy Hilton, Sam Neuville, Sam Tyfield and Sonja Petersen.

Everyone else – where would I be without you? Thanks to my parents and sister, Susan James (who had to work a lot harder due to my inexperience), Peter Schiazza (the handsomest, most hardworking photographer ever), everyone at 2 Bedford Row (ridiculously supportive in all I do), The Space Hijackers (for stopping me from getting old before my time), and everyone I've ever taught to knit (they taught me how to write this book).

Dedication

This book is dedicated to

Sureshbhai Rambhai Patel and
Hasuben Sureshbhai Patel

My Parents

Jai Shree Krishna

Contents

Welcome
to the wonderful world of knitting

Hello, my name is Aneeta

I'm your knitting teacher. Have you ever knitted before? Not since you were little? Can't really remember anything? Well, don't worry – we are going to start from scratch. I have been teaching knitting classes for a few years now; I teach men, women and children of all races, ages and backgrounds. The one thing every one of these people has in common is a desire to 'make something'.

These days, our lives can be so fast-paced and the pressure to succeed (in material terms) so unrelenting that often there is little time left over for nurturing our creative and emotional wellbeing. Knitting is a craft that can be used as a creative outlet – you can produce something unique and original, and relax at the same time! I have a tendency to get a bit Zen about it, but I do truly believe that every ounce of creativity generated keeps the planet spinning. For me, one of the best things about knitting is that the whole exercise is packed full of 'instant gratification'. Within a short time, with a relatively small amount of effort, anyone can produce something wearable, practical and beautiful.

Knitting is a fantastic creative force that you can harness to produce anything from a footie scarf for your father to a wrist-cuff for your wannabe rock-star little brother. Imagine the pleasure of someone asking where you bought that pretty scarf and being able to nonchalantly say, 'I made it myself'. I hope that this book will start you on a lifetime addiction to knitting.

Knitty Gritty has been designed especially for absolute knitting-newcomers. If you follow these workshops and patterns carefully from beginning to end you will gain a solid grounding in basic knitting techniques and you will complete some very simple, enjoyable pieces of knitting as you go. If you are an 'advanced beginner' (you already understand the basics), then you can dip into the different workshops and projects to brush up your skills, learn new techniques, and knit some gorgeous projects along the way.

In the above image, both squares have been knitted using the same number of stitches and rows. They are different sizes because they were knitted on different-sized needles

The Science Bit

The absolute beginner will find knitting patterns hugely confusing, almost as though they are written in a foreign language (which of course they have – Knit!). This book provides a simple and straightforward translation and simplification service for beginners, as well as easy-to-knit patterns for items you will be happy to wear, use or to give as special presents.

You will probably learn a variety of different methods eventually, but the main focus of this book is just to help you begin to knit, so you can learn how to start (and how to stop!), create some finished knitting of your own, and, most importantly, enjoy the process without becoming bogged down in or overwhelmed by technicalities. This way you will gradually familiarise yourself with the basic techniques as a good grounding for more advanced and skilful knitting in the future.

In knitting there is not always just one right way to do something; if you asked twelve knitters to show you how to cast on, they could each feasibly show you a different way. So the techniques I teach you in this book won't provide final answers and definitive rules, they are simply the methods my beginner students find the easiest and most useful. I think that showing one straightforward method is more constructive than bombarding you with too many confusing choices – please bear this in mind when you are asking advice of other knitters (or sharing your own wisdom further on in your knitting career)!

Tension

A tension or gauge square is knitted to make sure that you are knitting to the same dimensions as the pattern designer intended, and to ensure that your garment knits up to the exact size required. Tension and gauge are very important when making precisely fitted garments.

If you are working from a true beginner's pattern (rather than a pattern for an advanced beginner who already knows the basics), knitting a tension square should not always be necessary because:

- a tension square will take so long for an absolute beginner to knit that they may become disheartened at having to work so hard before even getting stuck into a project (especially if there is more than one tension square to be knitted);

- a true beginner's pattern will not need to be made to such rigid and precise dimensions; and

- a beginner's knitting tension will be constantly changing as they get used to the process and the stitches so a tension square wouldn't be completely accurate.

I have not stated precise tensions in any of the projects in this book – only yarn weight and needle size. One of the consequences of this is that two different knitters may get two different-sized projects, so remember that all stated final sizes are approximate. For example, the child's hat may fit any head from age 3-10 years, depending on the child's head and the knitter. The key is not to get stuck with trying to make exact sizes at this stage; you should be enjoying learning a new skill and making fun things. As you gain more confidence and experience, you will find more demanding or precise patterns easier to cope with. This is why I haven't included any patterns in this book that need to fit exactly.

You will notice that I sometimes include a different needle to that suggested on a ball of yarn – there is a good reason for this. Each yarn will have an optimum needle size for knitting – this is where the tension comes in. If you use the suggested needle, the knitting should come out at the size shown on the gauge square on the yarn label. This means your knitting will work out at the same size as a pattern in that suggested gauge. However, as I have already mentioned, one of the things I notice with all beginner knitters is that their tension varies constantly throughout their work. Even during the knitting of a single scarf, a beginner's stitches will not be consistent. This is perfectly normal, and will be corrected with practice. There is no huge problem with inconsistent tension when you are just starting out, but it does mean that even if you knit an item following every single instruction correctly your knitting might still end up uneven in some places. It won't happen forever, just while you are getting used to the process of knitting. Carry on cheerfully, remembering that you are a beginner, and it will come right in time.

As this book has been written specifically for beginners, I have purposely designed patterns in which the tension won't make or break the work. This is why you'll notice that there aren't any adult garments – with adult clothes, a precise fit is often necessary, and this means knitting with an even tension throughout. With the patterns in this book, it won't matter terribly if your tension is a bit of a rollercoaster – it shouldn't make too much difference to the final piece. Always remember: knitting should be relaxing and you are supposed to be having fun!

Even in the baby and child cardigans, I have designed the patterns to have a bit of extra stretch in them (by suggesting a slightly larger needle size than that on the yarn label) so you shouldn't have a problem in making them fit the child. If anything, I have written the cardigan pattern a little on the large side – it will fit the child eventually. If in doubt about patterns for babies and children, always choose the size up.

When choosing yarn for the patterns, I have given suggestions, but I have purposely left the yarn choice up to you. The yarn weight and approximate amounts needed are shown, but you should realise that the yarn weight is a sufficient guide for the time being and finding specific yarns is something you can focus on a little later. You can work within your own budget, and have fun rummaging around yarn shops and websites to see what's out there.

The Tried-and-Tested Guarantee

There are stacks of beautiful knitting books out there, written by very talented knitwear designers and accomplished knitters. However, the main complaint I hear repeatedly wailed by my absolute beginner students is that these books often assume the reader already knows how to knit. As well as not assuming anything of the sort in this book, I have also incorporated a 'Tried-and-Tested' guarantee with my workshops and patterns – genuine beginner knitters have knitted up all of these patterns (and they haven't been shy with their constructive criticism and clever suggestions for improving the patterns for beginners' use). I hope that this road-tested approach means that you will be able to use this book productively and happily.

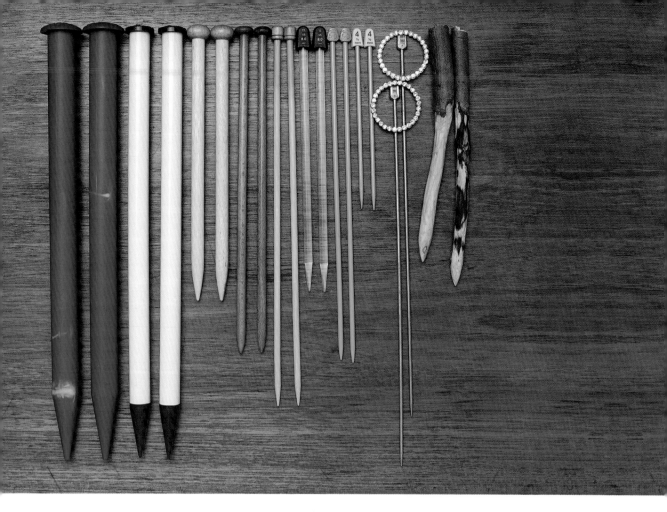

Your essential knit kit

Needles

Needles these days come in all shapes, sizes, materials and colours; I have a gorgeous hand-whittled pair and a glamorous diamanté pair! Most of you will have seen metal knitting needles; they are the most easily available and often the least expensive. These days, bamboo needles are very popular - they can be a little more expensive than metal needles, but they have a lovely natural feel to them, a little bit of give and, for prolific knitters, they are said to be less likely to cause hand pain. For beginners, bamboo needles are better than metal as they are less slippery, so there is less chance of dropping stitches. However, if you find that you knit very tightly, the slipperiness of metal needles might help you loosen up your stitches. For variety and help in finding your preferred needle type, also try: casein, plastic, wooden, and any others that you can easily get your hands on.

The best piece of advice here is: experiment. Every time you buy knitting needles, try them in a different material. Everyone has personal preferences and you will find your own favourites in time.

Gadgets and Gizmos

You don't need to spend a fortune to become a knitter: a ball of yarn and a pair of needles will get you going. However, if you can see yourself knitting into the future, here are a few basics you might want to collect (these are all used throughout the patterns in this book): yarn, knitting needles, darning needles, crochet hook, scissors, pencil, cable needle, tape measure. If you have these basic tools, you can acquire additional extras as and when your new projects require them.

Yarn

These days yarn is available in a huge number of materials, colours and weights. Gone are the days when hand-knitting meant suffering inside itchy lurid green acrylic sweaters! Yarn now comes in all sorts of exotic variations, as you will see when you spend some time browsing in yarn stores; this is one of my favourite pastimes, but with so many wonderful yarns on offer the longer you look the more difficult choosing just one yarn to take home becomes!

Alongside the patterns in this book, I have included suggestions for appropriate weights of yarn to use. These are mostly standard weights – just remember that the names may differ depending on which country you are shopping in. If you go into your local yarn store and ask for the weight of yarn you need, they will know exactly what you are talking about and direct you to the correct shelf of goodies.

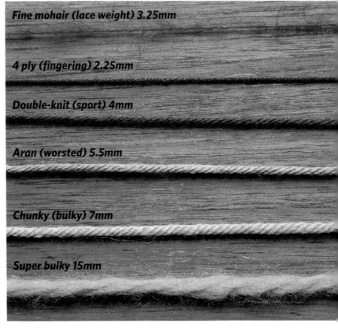

Fine mohair (lace weight) 3.25mm

4 ply (fingering) 2.25mm

Double-knit (sport) 4mm

Aran (worsted) 5.5mm

Chunky (bulky) 7mm

Super bulky 15mm

UK name (US name) suggested needle size

The Slipknot

Without the ever-necessary slipknot you won't get very far at all with your knitting so practice, practice and practice it again - this is the one thing you are not allowed to forget!

For the girl guides, boy scouts and sailors amongst you this won't be necessary, but for the rest, here's how to make a slipknot.

Step 1. Make the yarn into an **upside-down U-shape**. Please note that at all times I'm holding onto the ends of the yarn with my fingers – this will keep everything in place as you are making your slipknot.

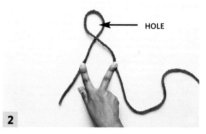

Step 2. Fold the upside down U over so the **right side goes over the left**.

Step 3. Fold (where the yarn crosses over itself) the **hole over the left** side.

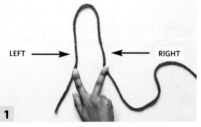

Step 4. Pull out the centre section (remembering to keep hold of the ends) – this is a slipknot!

Step 5. Once you have your slipknot, place it onto the needle (slide the needle upward through the segment you pulled out above – totally foolproof – I hope!) and pull tight. You know that it has worked if the slipknot undoes when you pull on the two ends of the yarn. This is your first stitch.

How to Cast On

'Casting on' is the phrase used to describe making the first row of stitches on your needle, so that you can begin knitting. If you asked a dozen different knitters how to cast on, you'd get a dozen different answers. My sister, who I taught to knit, now prefers a different cast-on method to me.

There's no right or wrong way, but I've chosen the method I've been teaching for years. This is the most 'tried and tested' part of this book!

Step 1. Start with the slipknot on your **left-hand needle**. This is your first stitch.

Step 2. Pick it up. Pick up this first stitch with the right-hand needle – insert the right-hand needle into the stitch from the bottom, keep the **needles crossed left over right**.

Knitter's Notes

You will notice that I often talk about the 'back,' 'middle' or 'front' of your work. Front is closest to you, back is furthest away, and middle is in between the two knitting needles when they are crossed over.

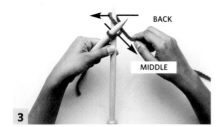

Step 3. Back and then middle. Hold both the needles between the thumb and first two fingers of your left hand – this leaves your right hand free. Wrap the long end of the yarn to the **back** of both needles and through the **middle** of the needles.

Step 4. Underneath and to the front. Bring the tip of the right-hand needle **underneath** the loop on the left needle and to the **front** of the work.

CONTINUE...

How to Cast On *continued...*

Step 5. Stand both needles up straight.
Hold onto the stitches with your thumbs.

Step 6. Left needle up the right stitch.
Insert the tip of the left hand needle up the stitch on the right needle.

Step 7. Then release the right needle.
Pull the right-hand needle out of the work and pull on the long end of the yarn. This is your second stitch.

Continue until you have cast on as many stitches as you require to start your knitting. Please note that with this method of casting on, your work in will 'grow' in width approximately 50% between the cast-on row and the first knitted row. By this I mean that the work itself will end up wider than the width of the cast-on row (e.g., in the picture on the right, the cast-on row measures 8cm. In the first knitted row, this width will grow to approximately 12cm). This is important to remember when you are knitting your first scarf. If at this stage you are unhappy with your cast on, undo it and start again – it's all good practice!

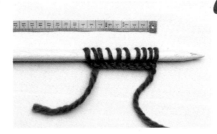

The work will grow in width by approximately 50% between the cast on row and first knitted row.

❝**Words of Wisdom**
I'm sure that you are a bright, successful human being. But remember that you are now learning something completely new that might be totally outside of your previous experience. KNITTING DOES NOT COME NATURALLY! It is easy when you know how, but until then, don't be hard on yourself. Relax, engage some extra patience, and stop for frequent cups of tea and chocolate biscuits. And embrace the joy of undoing your work and starting all over again – just remember that you are getting extra use out of your yarn and needles❞

Questions & Answers

Why does the work 'grow' in the first row?
I don't know – it's just a feature of this particular cast-on method.
The work will grow in width by approximately 50% between the cast on row and first knitted row.

How to Knit

This is the most basic stitch you can learn; using this you can be happily knitting in no time.

In a knitting pattern, knit is abbreviated to K. So K1, would mean 'knit one stitch.' And K1 row would mean 'knit one row.'

Start knitting here...!

Start with your cast on stitches in your left hand and the empty needle in your right hand.

Handy HINT

Wrap the long end of the yarn once around the index finger of your right hand. Everyone has their own way of holding the yarn, but until you find yours, this is the easiest way of keeping the yarn in the correct place; it will also help even out your tension.

1

Step 1. Pick it up. Insert the tip of the right needle into the stitch on the left needle – from the bottom to the top. Keep needles crossed over left over right.

2

Step 2. Back and then the middle. Holding both the needles in your left hand (between the thumb and first two fingers) wrap the long end of the yarn to the back of both needles (away from you) and then through the middle of the needles (back towards you).

3

Step 3. Underneath and then to the front. Bring the tip of the right hand needle under the first loop on the left needle.

4a

Step 4. Release. Gently push the stitch on the left needle off using your left thumb.

4b

Repeat these moves until all the stitches are on the right needle and the left needle is empty. Then swap the needles in your hands so that the stitches are once again in your left hand and the empty needle is in your right hand. Carry on knitting in the same way.

Rule Number One

At the end of every row – COUNT YOUR STITCHES! This is a hard and fast rule for all beginners. It will mean the difference between an even, tidy piece of knitting and something very scary.

CONTINUE...

Handy HINT

Remember to work away from the tip of the needle. This will help your tension and technique. Imagine the needle as having a thin part (at the tip) and a fat part (the main length of the needle). If you work too much towards the thin part, there is a risk a) of all the stitches slipping off the needles; and b) that when eventually you move the stitches down to the fat part of the needle, they will be too tight. A bit like buying an outfit that's too small for you! So at each step, move the stitch down to the fat part of the needle. This might seem like a lot of sliding the stitch up and down, but it'll be worth it in the long run!

Rule Number Two

Never put down your knitting in the middle of a row. Always finish knitting the row before you set your knitting aside or once you pick it up again you will inevitably start knitting in the wrong direction and make mistakes. If the phone rings, try to leave it – they'll call you back or leave you a message!

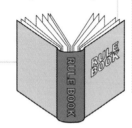

The Knit Mantra

Step 1 Pick it up
Step 2 Back and then middle
Step 3 Underneath and to the front
Step 4 Release

Make this your mantra. Say the words to yourself as you are knitting so you don't forget to work each step in order. Use your patience. If you take the time at this stage to work each stitch precisely and carefully, you are less likely to make mistakes and more likely to create beautiful, tidy knitting.

Garter stitch

If you knit every row, the stitch you create is called garter stitch. This looks the same on both sides and is the perfect stitch to knit your first project with.

Garter Stitch. Rowan Big Wool and 15mm knitting needles used in this picture

Casting off

'Casting off' (or 'binding off') is the term used for finishing a piece of knitting so that your knitting can live independently of its needles. You must securely cast off the stitches from the needles so that your work will not unravel.

Knitter's Notes

Knitting tension: Whether you are a 'tight' or 'loose' knitter, when casting off always keep your stitches looser than you usually would. This will stop the work from puckering at the cast-off edge. A tight cast-off can look ugly and will spoil your knitting.

Handy HINT

If you find it hard to keep your cast off loose, try using a knitting needle slightly bigger than you used in the rest of your knitting (in your right hand) to cast off with.

Step 1. Knit two stitches.

Step 2. Insert the tip of the left needle down first stitch.

Step 3. Using your left index finger to guide the tip of the right needle.

Lift the first stitch over the second stitch and the right needle.

Keeping the long end of the yarn secure will help.

Step 4. Remember to release the stitch you lifted over the right needle. You will then have one stitch on the right needle.

Step 5a. Then knit one more stitch so that you have two stitches on your right knitting needle again. Then repeat the move of using the left needle to lift the lower stitch on the right needle over the upper stitch and off the left needle.

Remember that you should only have one or two stitches on the right needle at any point during casting off.

CONTINUE...

Step 5b. You are now casting off.

Step 6. Keep casting off until you have just one stitch left on one needle and the other needle is empty. Then cut the yarn.

Step 7. Pass the cut end of the yarn through the last stitch left on your knitting needle, remove the knitting needle and pull tight.

Step 8. Then weave this end in securely using a crochet hook – if you don't, your knitting will surely unravel.

Notice how the cast-off edge looks. One side has an edge that looks like a 'plait.' This now counts as the wrong side of your work – even if you've been knitting a double-sided stitch like garter stitch. You shouldn't be able to see the 'plait' edge from the right side. (Of course, if you have been making a garter stitch scarf it will be impossible to hide the edge, so don't worry about it.) This advice is just for projects that have an inside and outside.

When casting off on a stocking stitch piece of knitting, always cast off with the wrong side (purl side) facing you. Otherwise, the plait will form on the right side of your work; this may seem a very small point, but this kind of attention to detail will take you a long way towards giving your work a professional finish.

Questions & Answers

When casting off on the wrong side of a stocking stitch piece, should I be using purl stitch to cast off?

No this won't matter, as you will be casting off on the wrong side, so your plait edge won't be seen. But when you are using knit/purl combinations such as a rib stitch you will have to cast off slightly differently. Don't worry about this right away; we will cover this further on in the book.

My cast-off edge looks very tight and 'bunches' up so that my work doesn't lie flat. What am I doing wrong?

This means you are casting off too tightly. When casting off, try to keep your tension and the stitches on your right knitting needle much looser than you would when knitting normally. If you have trouble making these stitches looser, try casting off using a knitting needle one size bigger than the needles you have used in the rest of the work.

How to add a new colour or start new ball of yarn

When you come to the end of a ball of yarn, you will have to add a new ball in order to carry on knitting. To do this, you follow exactly the same procedure as for adding a new colour to include a stripe in your knitting.

The illustrated instructions show the adding of new yarn as if to stripe – this is so you can see the change more easily, but it is exactly the same as if you had just come to the end of one ball and wanted to continue with more yarn of the same colour.

It's best to do a colour change at the end of a row, so make sure you do this while there is still enough of the old yarn left to add new yarn easily (about 10cm).

Please note: When you are adding new yarn of the same colour you can add it to either side of your knitting; when adding a new yarn of a different colour, you must add it to the same side each time (so that all your loose ends are on the same side and the work now has a right side (rs) and a wrong side (ws).

Step 1. Lay your work out and make a 'cross' shape with the new yarn under the old yarn.

Step 2. Tie the new yarn into a knot with itself, with the old yarn lying inside that knot. Don't tie the knot too tightly.

Step 3. Slide the new yarn knot up until it touches the knitting needle.

Step 4. Pull the ends of the new yarn to tighten the knot.

Step 5. Then simply start knitting with the new yarn.

Step 6. Where you have changed/added yarn, your work will have loose yarn ends, like little tails. These have to be woven into your knitting to secure them and stop your knitting from unravelling.

Weaving in ends

Weaving in the ends of yarn in your knitting will give you a tidy professional finish and stop your work unravelling, which is what would happen if you just cut these ends off.

You will need a crochet hook. Any size of crochet hook close to the size of knitting needle you are working with is fine – it doesn't have to be exactly the same.

If you have been knitting a colour stripe, weave the ends into the wrong side of the work (as shown in these images). If your work is all the same colour, you should still use the wrong side to weave into; and weave into the same side all the way through the piece. (Of course, a scarf doesn't have to have a wrong and a right side; if this is the case, just choose any side to weave into and stick with this choice.)

Step 1. Insert the crochet hook into the stitch next to the end you are about to weave in. Hold the 'hook' of the crochet hook facing away from you and towards the work.

Step 2. Wrap the end of the yarn **over and then under** the crochet hook.

Step 3. Use the hook to pull the end of the yarn through the stitch on your knitting.

Step 4. Once the yarn has been pulled right through the stitch, repeat the move on the next four stitches in the row.

Step 5. Cut the woven end of the yarn close to the knitted piece. Now you have woven in the blue yarn along the blue stitches.

Step 6. Next, weave in the pink yarn along the adjacent pink stitches. Of course, if all your yarn is the same colour, you will just choose the row nearest the cut end of the yarn to weave into.

Step 7. This is the back of your knitting: wrong side = ws

Your work now has a lovely professional finish!

The ends of yarn at the cast-on and cast-off edges should also be woven into your work. If you don't do this (especially at the cast-off edge), your work will eventually unravel and this is not only disheartening, but also difficult to fix and extremely messy!

How to purl

Purl is the second stitch you need to learn. In a knitting pattern, purl is abbreviated to P. So 'P1' means 'purl one stitch.' And 'P 1 row' means 'purl one row.'

The first thing to note is this: when you knit, the yarn is held to the back of the work, and when you purl, the yarn is held to the front.

Purl with yarn at front

Knit with yarn at back

1

Step 1. Pick it up. Insert the tip of the right needle into the stitch on the left needle – from top to the bottom. Keep needles crossed over right over left. Your yarn should be at the front of the work.

2

Step 2. Middle and then front. Holding both the needles in your left hand (between thumb and first two fingers), wrap the long end of the yarn through the middle of the needles and then to the front of the needles.

3a

Step 3. Underneath and to the back.

3b

Take the tip of the right hand needle under the first loop on the left needle and to the back of the left needle.

4

Step 4. Release. Gently push the stitch on the left needle off, using your left thumb.

Repeat these moves all the way to the end of the stitches on the left needle so that you have purled all the stitches onto the right needle. Then swap the needles in your hands so that the stitches are once again in your left hand and the empty needle is in your right hand – ready for the next row.

Questions & Answers

What happens if I purl every row?

Your work will look the same as if you knit every row (garter stitch), but will take a bit longer as most people are slower at purling than knitting. I've never come across a pattern that instructs the knitter to purl every row.

Stocking Stitch

If you purl one row, then knit the next row, then keep swapping the rows between knit and purl, the pattern you create is called stocking stitch.

This stitch is not double-sided; it has a right side (rs) and a wrong side (ws). The right side is the side you knitted and the wrong side is the side you purled.

Stocking stitch. Rowan Big Wool and 15mm needles used in this picture

Because both sides are different, the work will curl up at all ends (as you can see in the photo below). This makes it unsuitable for scarves as they will curl up into tubes. Of course, there is always the chance that you might actually want to make a tubey-scarf, in which case you should get splendid results with stocking stitch.

Knit and purl stitches are the basis of all knitting. Now you know how to knit and purl, we will move onto using different combinations of these stitches to create all sorts of wonderful patterns later in the book.

Questions & Answers

I'm using stocking stitch and I've forgotten which stitch I'm supposed to do for the next row.

The best way to do this is to keep a note of your rows on a piece of paper as you are working. If you haven't been doing this, there is a simple way to work out which row to work next. Hold the needles in your hands as if were about to start your row. The knitting will be in your left hand and the empty needle in your right hand. Look at the side of the work that is facing you. You should be using the same stitch as that facing you, e.g., if the knit side of the work is facing you: knit. If the purl side is facing you: purl. Now for little memory trick: the purl side looks like waves. This reminds me of the ocean... where you find pearls (purl stitch). The knit side looks like, well, 'knitting'.

Mistakes

This is a very difficult section to write, because every mistake is different. If I delve too deeply into all the potential knitting mistakes you might make there would be no room in this book for any patterns!

Remember that you are making something lovingly by hand – you are not a machine, so mistakes happen. Learn to embrace your mistakes as part of making something original and individual. Also, just realising that you have made a mistake is half the battle already won. So, I am going to concentrate just on a few of the mistakes that crop up most frequently in my knitting classes.

Firstly, you must always follow Rule Number One: count your stitches at the end of every row. If you are doing this, you will immediately know if you have right number of stitches, too many, or too few.

Too many stitches
Most beginners end up with too many stitches. The official remedy is to 'frog' your knitting; this is the term used for undoing your work and starting again. However, this can be disheartening for a beginner and I think it is not always necessary when a sneaky little move can put you back on track! I hardly ever recommend 'frogging' to a beginner, as most beginners' mistakes won't happen once you are more used to knitting.

The last stitch looks as if it hasn't been knitted
That's because it hasn't. You can see that the yarn is engaged in the last but one stitch, but not the last stitch.

To fix this, hold the work in your hands so the stitches are all on your right needle and then pass the last (un-knitted) stitch back onto the left needle (without doing anything else to it).

Then treat that stitch as the last stitch on your row and knit it as normal. You will now notice that the yarn is engaged correctly on the last stitch.

One extra stitch at the beginning (at the beginning of the row)
A mistake that beginners often make is holding the yarn in the wrong place at the beginning of a row.

On this piece of knitting, there are eleven stitches when there should be ten. This is because the yarn is in the wrong place. All that you need to do is bring the yarn over the knitting needle to the front of the work and the extra stitch will disappear.

This mistake happens because of the baggy loop at the beginning of the row. Beginners' questions often feature this baggy loop - I don't know why it's there! But if you notice, it disappears in your knitting. It will only ever appear on the row you are currently working on. So don't worry about it, just ignore it – it's quite happy where it is!

CONTINUE...

Too many stitches (in the middle of the row)

If you have too many stitches, it will probably be because you haven't been following the steps to knit each stitch precisely enough. You will notice that two of the stitches look as if they are crossed over.

Crossed over stitches and one extra stitch when counting.

Knit the next row until you get to the mistake. Then pick up these crossed-over stitches together as if they were one. This will turn the two stitches into one, thus correcting the extra stitch.

How did I make that 'cross over' mistake?

 ✕

You created this mistake simply by losing a little concentration when knitting and not picking up the stitch precisely – remember that knitting in front of the telly is a joy still to come for now!

 ✓

Instead of picking up the stitch (you are about to knit) cleanly and precisely, you picked up the loop under the stitch by mistake. This isn't a huge mistake, but one that can be avoided with a little more concentration. With experience, you will notice the minute you do it; eventually you will just stop doing it altogether.

So that covers extra stitches – but beginners worry more about the infamous 'dropped stitch.' This can happen easily if you aren't working towards the fat part of the needle or if you aren't gentle when releasing your last stitch. Left to their own devices, dropped stitches would form a ladder like a snagged stocking, but they can be picked up with a little dexterity and a crochet hook and coerced back into line with the others.

Garter stitch dropped stitch

Step 1. So you've dropped a stitch and it's laddering. Don't panic, just try to fix this as soon as you notice it.

Step 2. Insert your crochet hook into the dropped stitch and keep the ladder to the front of the dropped stitch.

Step 3a. Hook the crochet hook onto the ladder and pull it through the dropped stitch.

Step 3b. That ladder then becomes the dropped stitch.

Step 4. Keep 'climbing the ladder' through each dropped stitch until you get back to the current row of knitting. Then put the final dropped stitch onto the left hand knitting needle and keep knitting the row.

Stocking stitch dropped stitch

Step 1. I find it easiest to fix a dropped stitch on a stocking stitch piece of knitting with the right side of the work facing me.

Step 2. Insert the crochet hook into the dropped stitch – with stocking stitch keep the ladder behind the dropped stitch.

Step 3. Hook the crochet hook onto the ladder behind the dropped stitch and pull it through to the front of the dropped stitch.

Step 4. Keep 'climbing the ladder' through each dropped stitch until you get back to the current row of knitting. Then put the final dropped stitch onto the left hand knitting needle and keep knitting the row.

These are not, by any means, all the mistakes it is possible to make in knitting – almost every knitter will invent a new mistake all their very own. However, these are the mistakes that I see most commonly with beginner students, and learning how to fix them will give you a better understanding of knitting and make you a more accomplished knitter later on. If all else fails and you just can't fix your knitting, simply ask for help. There's always a more experienced knitter around every corner.

Handy HINT

One of my beginner students has a memorable way of dealing with imperfections in her knitting. She simply sews a decorative button or sequin over the offending blemish. As a result, her knitting is always beautifully unique and quirky with no mistakes in sight!

Chunky Scarf

Now it's time to start getting excited – you are about to knit your first garment. Knitting a scarf is the first project most knitters take on; I hope it will be the start of a long and enjoyable journey into knitting for you.

This first project will be quick and easy to knit. It will give you essential practice in making the basic 'knit' stitch. The important thing is not worry too much about how it looks or any uneven-ness in your stitches or cast on/off. It's just important for you to know that you can start making something immediately with your newfound skills, and that you are learning so much more with each stitch. Don't forget the pleasure you will get from telling people you made it yourself!

Bulky yarn and big needles mean that your first project will be knitted up and ready to wear in no time

Chunky scarves are not just for grown ups – this is Wendy 'Fusion' an aran-weight yarn that changes colours by itself and knits up on 6mm needles

Colinette's 'Point 5' yarn changes colours and thickness every few cenimetres – a very hard-working yarn

Rule Number Three

Try to knit at least two rows once a day. This should fit into the busiest of schedules; the benefit being that you get some practice every day. For beginners this will mean that you remember how to knit quicker and easier than if you don't pick up your knitting for weeks at a time.

Choosing yarn and needles

I haven't given a specific yarn for you to use for your scarf, as I want you to be able to have a look around the yarn shops, learn about what's available and make your first design decision! I always recommend that beginners choose a thicker yarn and big fat knitting needles so that their first project grows quickly and is finished in good time for added satisfaction. This will help you feel positive about beginning your second project.

For the beginner's scarf, it's best to use only garter stitch. This does not mean that the scarf has to look dull - far from it. There are so many exciting yarns available these days that you can really 'make the yarn work for you.'

Two pairs of hands make yarn winding easier

Winding yarn

Most yarns come already wound into neat balls (or skeins) that you can use immediately. However, more and more yarns these days come in hanks that need to be wound into balls before knitting – if you don't do this you will end up in an awful tangle. The reason it comes in hanks is that this is how it is usually dyed (particularly hand-dyed yarn), and many yarns look more attractive displayed in hanks rather than balls. Beginners often find it a bit tricky to wind the yarn from hanks into useable balls. Some tips I can offer you are:

- Make sure you have an extra pair of hands to hold the yarn;

- Try to wind the yarn into an even ball by turning the ball as you create it;

- If you really have trouble making a ball, get a tennis ball and wrap the yarn around it, making sure you cover the tennis ball evenly – this is the best method for slippery silk yarns; and

- Persevere – knitting with balls will be infinitely easier than trying to knit from a hank.

Knitter's Notes

Reading a yarn label
The yarn label will tell you what size needles to use. For this project, this is a good indication of what is suitable – I suggest nothing that uses needles smaller than 6mm. The yarn label will also give the weight of your yarn, washing instructions, and how much yarn is in the ball.

Remember:

Aran, chunky, super bulky, or 'big' yarns will work best. Useful names are: Rowan 'Big Wool', Sirdar 'Bigga', Debbie Bliss 'Cashmerino Super Chunky', Colinette 'Point 5.' Once you take a look at these, you'll start to get the idea and can work within your price range to choose a yarn for your first project.

Shop around – there are some beautiful organic and hand-dyed yarns available. And it's not all 'wool' – look out for silk, cotton, alpaca, and more.

Don't choose anything too fine or fluffy. The pretty ribbon and mohair yarns might be tempting, but it's impossible to see the stitches and to undo mistakes. Save these yarns until you have more experience with knitting!

Two or three balls of yarn should be enough for your scarf, depending, of course, on how long you want it to be. It's always better to buy more rather than less; you can always return the unused ball, donate it to someone else or, better still, save it in your 'stash' for future projects.

START KNITTING

1 Cast on the number of stitches required. Remember the general rule that the width of your knitting will grow by 50% between the cast-on row and the first knitted row. It is completely up to you how wide your scarf is. My only suggestion is that if you knit a few rows and you find your scarf is too wide or narrow, start again. I want you to be happy with your first project. And if you've chosen according to my instructions, your yarn should be thick enough to knit up so quickly that starting again will hardly slow you down at all!

2 Garter stitch (knit every row) until scarf measures long enough to keep you warm.

3 Cast off loosely. Weave in all your ends.

Wear with pride or give as a thoughtful gift.

Finishing options

Tassels

You have finished your scarf – now it's time for tassels. These are an easy way to apply a fun and funky finish to your scarf; and if, as a beginner, you aren't happy with your cast on and cast off edges, it's a sneaky way of hiding them until you've had a bit more practice!

Also:

- Vary your yarn.

- Experiment with needle sizes. If you use a much bigger needle than recommended with your yarn, your knitting will have an open lacy weave.

- Add tassels.

- Knit in some stripes. Add these in the same way you would add a new ball of yarn.

- Weave some ribbon through your finished knitting with a darning needle for a pretty touch.

- Add pom-poms to the ends.

Making tassels

1

Cut lengths of yarn twice as long as the length you want your finished tassels to be.

2

Fold the cut tassel-yarn in half. Insert a crochet hook into the edge of your scarf, hook it onto the folded end of the tassel-yarn, and pull the folded end through the edge of the scarf.

3

Then take the two ends of the tassel-yarn, fold them over and bring them through the loop you just hooked through the scarf. Pull tight and there's your tassel.

Keep going along the cast on and cast-off edges of your scarf.

Decreasing Workshop

The most basic way to decrease is by picking up two stitches and knitting them together. As you knit them, they become one stitch. When you count your stitches at the end of the row, you will have one fewer than you started with. The abbreviation for this is K2tog – also known as – knit two stitches together. What you are doing is turning two stitches into one stitch.

As with everything, there are several ways to decrease. This is the simplest way.

K2tog = Knit two stitches together

When you pick up the stitch to knit or purl it, instead of putting the tip of the right hand needle into just one stitch, insert it into the first and second stitch at the same time. Then complete the stitch as normal. You will immediately see that you have only one stitch transferred onto the right hand needle.

Remember: you won't always be asked to decrease at the beginning of a row. You can decrease in the same way in the middle, or at the end of a row.

You can practice decreasing with Project 3: Hats

Sewing-up Workshop

I always find sewing up my work the least fun part of knitting. After all, if I'd wanted to sew, I'd be learning to sew!

But learning to sew up your knitting is necessary for most things you'll want to make, and learning to do it correctly can be the difference between a professional piece of knitting and something less beautiful.

That said, don't worry if it doesn't look great immediately; like knitting, sewing takes practice. So here's how to do it.

Methods for sewing up knitting are different depending on the stitch you knitted with. Here you will learn three techniques: backstitch, garter mattress and stocking stitch mattress. If you are sewing up a piece that incorporates two different knitting stitches, or something that you are not sure of, use backstitch. If both your pieces

are knitted in garter or stocking stitch, then use the appropriate mattress stitch.

You will need a yarn/darning needle – this is like a normal sewing needle, but thicker and with a blunt point and a large hole so that the yarn will slip through it easily. When sewing up, you will use this darning needle and a matching yarn. I've used a contrasting colour yarn in my images so you can clearly see just how I have done it.

Backstitch

Backstitch is the easiest sewing-up stitch, and you should pick this one if you are in any doubt about which stitch to use.

This is one of the strongest stitches and also gives a neat finish with the least amount of hassle.

Start with the work laid out inside-out (right sides together). After sewing, you will turn it right side out and not be able to see your stitches.

Secure the yarn at the beginning of the section to be sewed. This can be done in the same way you would weave in the ends (see Weaving In on p.24).

Then remember: One step back, two steps forward.

The stitch starts from point 1. Push the needle down into the work one step back and bring the needle back to the front moving two steps forward.

When you have sewn all the way to the end, weave in your ends and turn the work right-side out.

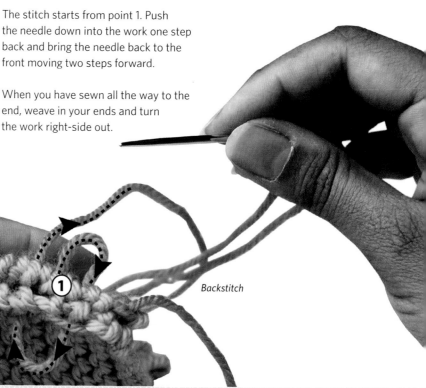

Backstitch

Stocking Mattress Stitch

This stitch will give you an invisible finish if both the pieces you are trying to knit are knitted in stocking stitch (knit one row, purl one row). It can also be used if you are knitting using a 'rib' stitch.

Start with the right side of the work facing you.

Step 1. Anchor the sewing yarn to your knitting by stitching up through one piece and down through the other. You can weave the ends in later.

Step 2. In between each column of stitches on the right side of your work, there is a horizontal 'bar.' You'll have to dig right in between the columns to find it. Insert your needle up the 'bar.'

Step 3. Then find the bar directly across from the first bar, on the other piece of knitting. Insert the darning needle up this bar.

Step 4. Keep working in this way on every stitch on each side of the piece you are sewing up. After you've sewn up a few bars, pull tightly on both ends of the sewing yarn.

Step 5. Your sewing yarn should virtually disappear.

Step 6. When you have sewn the entire piece (pulling the yarn tight as you go), turn your work to the wrong side and weave in your ends.

CONTINUE...

Garter Mattress Stitch

This stitch will give you an invisible finish if both the pieces you are trying to knit are knitted in garter stitch (knit every row). It can also be used if you are sewing up 'moss' or 'seed' stitch knitted pieces.

Start with the right side of the work facing you.

Step 1. Anchor the sewing yarn to your knitting by stitching up on the first piece and down through the next. You can weave the ends in later.

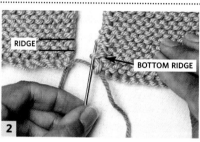

Step 2. You will notice that garter stitch is made up of 'ridges.' As you look at the image, there is a bottom ridge and a top ridge. We will be climbing these ridges like a ladder. Insert the darning needle up the bottom ridge.

Step 3. Then insert the darning needle up the top ridge on the other piece of knitting.

Step 4. Keep 'climbing' up your work using first the bottom ridge and then the top ridge.

Step 5. After a few stitches have been made, pull tight on both ends of the sewing yarn. Your sewing yarn should virtually disappear.

When you've sewn the entire seam, weave in your ends to the back of your work.

You can practice sewing up with Project 10: Hot Water Bottle Cover

Baby Booties

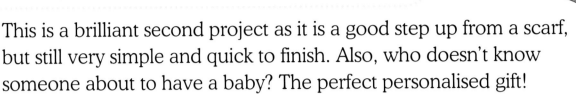

This is a brilliant second project as it is a good step up from a scarf, but still very simple and quick to finish. Also, who doesn't know someone about to have a baby? The perfect personalised gift!

This is a garter stitch bootie – this means that the stitch used is 'knit' for every row. There is no purl in this pattern.

As this is your first project using a pattern, I have broken it down fully so that you'll have images and help for each stage of the knitting. As you progress through the book, you'll learn more and more so that you'll need less help each time.

Overleaf are instructions written as they would be for a standard knitting pattern. Then I've broken the pattern down using images so you'll know what your knitting should look like at each stage.

YOU WILL NEED

50G DOUBLE-KNIT YARN
I suggest you choose one of the many specialist baby yarns available – Rowan 'Soft Baby' or Debbie Bliss 'Baby Cashmerino'

5MM KNITTING NEEDLES
For a smaller bootie, try using 4mm needles

DARNING NEEDLE
To sew up the bootie

HERE IS THE KNITTING PATTERN

ABBREVIATIONS:
K = Knit

K2tog = Knit two stitches together

St(s) = Stitch(es)

START KNITTING

1 Cast on 38 sts

2 Knit 12 rows

You will now start decreasing:

3 Row 13: K16, K2tog, K2, K2tog, K16.

Count 36 sts.

Row 14: K15, K2tog, K2, K2tog, K15.

Count 34 sts.

Row 15: K14, K2tog, K2, K2tog, K14.

Count 32 sts.

Row 16: K13, K2tog, K2, K2tog, K13.

Count 30 sts.

Row 17: K12, K2tog, K2, K2tog, K12.

Count 28 sts.

Row 18: K11, K2tog, K2, K2tog, K11.

Count 26 sts.

Row 19: K10, K2tog, K2, K2tog, K10. Count 24 sts.

4 Rows 20-27: Knit these next 8 rows.

5 Cast off loosely leaving a long end for sewing up (about 50cm).

6 To finish the bootie, fold it in half and sew up using the long cast-off end of yarn.

Choosing Yarn
A standard double-knit (DK) weight of yarn is used for this pattern, together with a needle one size bigger than normally used so that the booties are stretchy enough to fit various sizes of baby feet. The needle size should also help you avoid that typical beginners' problem: tight tension.

When choosing yarn, the assistants in the yarn store will help if you want them to; bear in mind that you are knitting for a baby, and choose your yarn accordingly. There are many lanolin-free, organic or cotton yarns available these days, and these are good options about if you are worried about allergies. Don't get anything too hot or scratchy – baby skin is very soft. Also, as pretty as they are, it's best to stay away from any yarn too fluffy or with bits or bobbles on it.

Remember Rule Number One
Count your stitches at the end of every row. This is very important to ensure that you are decreasing correctly, and that you end up with identical booties.

Handy HINT
If you tick off the rows as you knit them, you are more likely to get two booties the same size.

HERE IS THE PATTERN WITH PICTURES FOR EACH STAGE

START KNITTING

1

Cast on 38 sts

2

Knit 12 rows

3

Start decreasing

3a

When you have finished the decreasing rows, your bootie should start to take shape

4

Then knit 8 rows

5

Cast off loosely leaving a long end for sewing up (about 50cm)

6a

Hold the bootie right side out - so that the plait ridge of your cast off edge is on the inside

6b

Sew from the top of the bootie to the heel using garter mattress stitch

6c

When you get to the heel, turn the bootie inside out - so that the plait cast off edge is on the outside

6d

Then sew up the bottom of the bootie using backstitch

Weave in all your ends into the inside of the bootie.

Turn the bootie right-side-out, then knit another the same!

Handy HINT

If your cast off is too tight, the bootie will be hard to put on the baby's foot. To make your cast off looser, try using a knitting needle 1mm bigger than you used in the rest of your knitting to cast off with. (See Cast Off section, p21).

Questions & Answers

My bootie ended up enormous! What happened?
Some beginners knit very tightly and some knit very loosely. This means that your booties might turn out too big or too small or even different sizes each time. Knitting two the same comes with practice, but if your booties are too big, try making another using a 4mm knitting needle rather than the 5mm needle I've suggested.

The bootie on the left was knitted with 4mm knitting needles and the one on the right with 5mm needles. That is a demonstration of gauge – using different needles will alter the final piece of knitting you make: Bigger needles = bigger knitting. Smaller needles = smaller knitting.

Both my booties are different sizes!
What have I done wrong?
Nothing - this is just an example of your beginners' tension acting up. You can't expect to always knit evenly when you are a beginner – so don't worry if you have to knit three or more booties until you get two that match. And if you really have trouble, remember that babies won't complain too much!

Variation on the original bootie

Finishing options

These booties are very simple, but you can also add some variation to the last eight rows of the pattern if you want to. Here are just a few finishing options:

Run some ribbon through with a darning needle and tie it in a bow.

Instead of just plain garter stitch, try stocking stitch for a pretty rolled edge.

1x1 rib the last eight rows – see stitch patterns (p.48)

Knit more than 8 rows for a 'boot' look.

Stitch Patterns Workshop

Now that you know how to knit and purl, you can start using these two stitches in different combinations to create all sorts of new patterns.

The most important thing to remember with stitch patterns is that when you knit you hold the yarn to the back of the work, and when you purl hold the yarn to the front of the work.

If you are knitting and purling in the same row, you must move the yarn to the front and back between each knit and purl stitch. If you knit or purl with the yarn in the wrong place, the correct pattern won't appear in your work, and you'll end up with an extra twisted stitch. This will make more sense in practice, so let's move onto to the most basic of stitch combinations.

Knit with yarn at back

Purl with yarn at front

Handy HINT

Remember Rule Number One. Counting your stitches when working stitch patterns is essential and will ensure that your pattern stays accurate.

1 x 1 rib

'1 x 1 rib' means that you will be knitting one stitch, then purling one stitch, and repeating the k1, p1, sequence to the end of a row.

Begin with an even number of stitches. You will always start with a knit stitch and end with a purl stitch.

Step 1. Knit one stitch.
Step 2. Bring the yarn towards you to the front of the work, over the top, and through the middle of the needles. YF = Yarn Forward.

Step 3. Purl one stitch. The yarn will automatically be at the front after you purl a stitch.

Step 4. YB = Yarn Back. Pass the yarn to the back of the work, going over and in between the knitting needles.

Repeat steps 1, 2, 3 and 4 to the end of the row: knit one, yarn forward, purl one, yarn back, repeat from the beginning to the end of the row.

When this is written in a knitting pattern, the movement of the yarn forward and back between knit and purl stitches is taken as read, and won't be written in (unless it is for a reason in the pattern – see Eyelet Buttonholes on p.64).

The pattern would be written: K1, P1, rib, repeat to end.

This is what you should expect to see as you knit a 1 x 1 rib stitch. When stretched out, you can see the columns of knit and purl stitches. When the work is allowed to relax, the purl stitches disappear, and you can only see the knit stitches.

1x1 Rib.
To knit a practice square:
Cast on 20 stitches.
K1, P1, rib, repeat to end. Repeat this row until you have a practice square.

Questions & Answers

Help! I'm in the middle of a row and I've forgotten whether I should be knitting or purling!
This happens. All it takes is a momentary lapse of concentration. Look at the stitches you have already done on your right hand needle. Remember that the first stitch you knitted was a knit stitch, then count up the needle: knit one, purl one, knit one, purl one… oh yes…the next stitch is a knit stitch. Is my yarn at the back? Yes it is. Now keep going.

CONTINUE...

Stitch patterns *continued...*

Handy HINT

Look closely at your stitches, just where they meet the knitting needle. The purls and knits look different to one another. If you imagine them to be little people, the purls look like they are wearing little polo (turtle) neck sweaters (⌒), and the knits look like they are wearing a 'V' neck sweater. This is a great little trick to remind you where you are.

Questions & Answers

When will I need to use this stitch?
A rib stitch knits into a narrower and stretchier piece of knitting than garter or stocking stitch. It is often used for the collars and cuffs of knitted garments. Have a look at any sweaters you own – even on machine knitting, you will probably notice that the edges are knitted using a rib stitch.

Now that you understand that a knit stitch is made with the yarn held to the back of your work and a purl stitch is made with the yarn held to the front, you can use the stitches in all sorts of beautiful and interesting combinations. Try this one to test your newfound skills.

Now try 2 x 2 rib

To knit a practice square:

Cast on a multiple of four stitches. 20 is a good number for a practice square.

K2, P2, rib, repeat to end.

Moss Stitch

Cast on an odd number of stitches.
K1, P1, repeat to end.

If you start with an odd number of stitches, you will start and end with a knit stitch and your work will appear as one of my favourite stitches – moss (seed as it's sometimes known) stitch.

Stitch Patterns: Casting Off

If you have been knitting using a stitch pattern, for example, 1x1 rib, you must keep working this stitch pattern when you are casting off.

For 1x1 rib, this would mean:
K1, P1, cast off, K1, cast off, P1, cast off...and so on, remembering to move the yarn back and forward depending on whether you are knitting or purling the next stitch.

You will find more stitch patterns later in the book.

Knit Hats

After you've knitted a scarf, you will naturally start thinking of hats.

Baby hat with simple flower. See P.xx for flower instructions

Children's and adults' hats

Adult hat is suitable for either a man or woman

This pattern is for a double-knit yarn (perhaps in a yarn to match or complement your scarf). This pattern is for a garter stitch hat with a 1 x 1 rib border, and you will have three size options: baby, child and adult. The size of the final hat will depend on your knitting tension, but the patterns below cover the main sizes you might want to knit.

You will have a chance to use your new skills in stitch combinations and decreasing, and also a 'drawstring' finish which is useful for several other patterns in this book (and a pretty nifty way of finishing work as an alternative to casting off).

YOU WILL NEED

DOUBLE-KNIT YARN:
50G FOR BABY AND CHILD SIZES, 100G FOR ADULT HAT
(I have awful childhood memories of itchy hats – I always remember that when knitting a hat now. Rowan 'Pure Wool DK' or Debbie Bliss 'Cashmerino DK' are both warm and soft.)

5MM KNITTING NEEDLES

DARNING NEEDLE

Sizes

This pattern is an additional challenge in that it is written for three different sizes. This is one of the things that beginners can find confusing about knitting patterns, as it means that there is a lot of additional information included for sizes of garments that you don't need. If you have ever done any sewing from sized patterns you may be familiar with this problem.

As this pattern is for three different sizes, there will always be three sets of numbers. The first is for baby size, then child size, then adult size. The first size is written first, with the second two sizes following in brackets: Baby, (Child, Adult).

For example: K10 sts, (12 sts, 0 sts).

Translation:
• for the baby size you knit 10 stitches;
• for the child size you knit 12 stitches; and
• for the adult size you knit no stitches at all.

For consistency, even if no stitches have to be knitted, all three sets of instructions are shown. The pattern will also tell you how many stitches to count at the end of a decrease row.

Before you start knitting...

use a pencil to lightly circle all the numbers that you will need for the particular size of hat you are making This way you can simply ignore all the additional information.

ABBREVIATIONS:

K = Knit	
K2tog = Knit two stitches together	
St(s) = Stitch(es)	
Rep = Repeat	
1x1 Rib = Knit one stitch, purl one stitch	

(K1, K2tog) = when a sequence of stitches is bracketed, you have to repeat the entire bracketed section as many times as is written next to the bracketed section. For example: (K1, K2tog) 3 times = K1, K2tog, K1, K2tog, K1, K2tog. You can see why abbreviations are necessary in knitting patterns!

START KNITTING

Cast on 80 sts, (84 sts, 90 sts)
TRANSLATION: 80 sts for baby hat, 84 sts for child hat or 90 sts for adult hat.

1 1x1 rib border – Same for all 3 hat sizes:

K1, P1, rib, repeat to end. Repeat this rib row a total of 8 times. Keeping a tally of rows will help you with this.

2 Garter stitch (knit every row) until piece measures 13cm (15cm, 18cm) from beginning

Start decreasing:

1st Decrease:

(K1, K2tog) rep 26 times, (28 times, 30 times). K2 (K0, K0). Count 54 sts (56, 60).
TRANSLATION: (Knit 1 st, Knit 2 sts together), repeat the bracketed section 26 times for baby, (28 times for child, 30 times for adult). K2 sts (0, 0) - this means that you don't have to knit any stitches for the child and adult sizes). Count 54 sts (56, 60).

K1row – same for all three sizes.

2nd Decrease:

(K1, K2tog), rep 18 times, (18 times, 20 times). K0, (K2, K0). Count 36 sts, (38 sts, 40 sts).

K1row – same for all three sizes.

3rd Decrease:

(K1, K2tog), rep 12 times, (12 times, 13 times). K0, (K2, K1). Count 24 sts, (26 sts, 27 sts).

K1row – same for all three sizes.

4th Decrease:

(K1, K2tog), rep 8 times, (8 times, 9 times). K1, (K2, K0). Count 16 sts, (18 sts, 18 sts).

K1row – same for all three sizes.

5th Decrease:

(K1, K2tog), rep 5 times, (6 times, 6 times). K1, (K0, K0). Count 11 sts, (12 sts, 12 sts).

K1row – same for all three sizes.

6th Decrease:

(K1, K2tog), rep 3 times, (4 times, 4 times). K2, (K0, K0). Count 8 sts, (8 sts, 8 sts).

K1row – same for all three sizes.

1x1 rib border

Garter stitch main body of hat

Decrease until 8 stitches remain

CONTINUED

Drawstring finish (this is the same for all three hat sizes)

When you have finished your decreasing, cut the yarn leaving a long end. This end should measure 50-70cm, depending on which size hat you are making. Pay attention to this method; it will be used again later!

1 Thread the cut end of the yarn onto a darning needle. Insert the darning needle into the stitches on the knitting needle.

2 Pass the darning needle through the stitches remaining on the knitting needle, one by one, removing them from the knitting needle as they are secured by the yarn on the darning needle.

3 Pull the yarn tight.

4 Your piece of knitting should now naturally fall into a hat shape.

5 Sew it up using garter mattress stitch on the main body of the hat, and stocking mattress stitch on the border of the hat.

(See: Sewing-up workshop on p.38.) There is no right or wrong side to your hat before you start sewing it up, as the rib and garter stitches you've used are both double-sided and there is no cast-off edge.

When you've finished sewing up the hat, weave the ends of the yarn into the inside of the hat.

Finishing options

Pom-poms! Pom-poms are a fun addition to hats, scarves, booties and all sorts of knitted work. Most people remember making them at school; here's a quick refresher course.

YOU WILL NEED

CARDBOARD
(from a cereal packet – or any of a similar weight you might have lying around)

SCISSORS

YARN

DARNING NEEDLE
(you can manage without a needle, but it will make the process quicker and easier)

1

Cut two pieces of cardboard in a circle shape, with a smaller concentric hole cut out of the middle of both pieces. (The size of your pom-pom will depend on the dimensions of the cardboard circles.) Thread a long piece of yarn onto your darning needle.

2

Hold both cardboard circles together and start wrapping them in yarn – using the yarn on the darning needles will make this a bit easier. You'll have to keep re-threading your needle as making a pom-pom takes quite a bit of yarn.

3

Keep wrapping the yarn around the cardboard until the circle of card is completely covered. The more yarn you wrap, the fuller your pom-pom will be.

4

Push the wrapped yarn apart and insert your scissors in between the two circles of cardboard.

5

Start cutting the yarn, keeping your scissors inserted into the gap between the cardboard circles as a guide. This can be fiddly, with a risk of the cut pieces falling off through the hole – I find that laying the work flat on a table and supporting it with your other hand helps.

6

When you've cut all around the circle, slightly separate the cardboard pieces and slide a long piece of yarn into the space and then all the way around the circle.

7

Ease the cardboard circles apart, and tie the long piece of yarn into a tight knot around the 'waist' of the cut pieces.

8

Take the cardboard circles off the wrapped and cut yarn, pull really tight and tie a really, really tight knot so that none of the cut pieces escape your pom-pom.

Increasing Workshop

You have learned how to decrease; now you will learn how to increase. This is a very useful method for creating all sorts of shapes in your work.

As mentioned in previous chapters, there will be more than one way to increase – what I will teach you here is called a 'bar' increase. This is because you will be picking up what looks like a horizontal bar between the stitches. I call it the 'soup and scoop' method – you'll see why in a moment.

You can practice increasing with Project 4: Zig Zag Scarf

Increasing

In a knitting pattern, when you are asked to increase a stitch, you will read: 'M1.' This abbreviation means 'make one stitch.' The following instructions show how to 'M1' at the beginning of a row; when you have to M1 at the end of a row, you make the stitch just before the last stitch on the row. When you increase in the middle of a row, the pattern will tell you how many stitches to knit before you M1.

Step 1. Knit one stitch.

Step 2. Hold the needles apart and pull down on the work with the thumb and finger of your right hand. You will see a shape that resembles a bowl (of soup).

Step 3. Imagine the tip of the left hand needle to be a spoon. Scoop up the horizontal line of yarn (the soup) from the back to the front (towards your mouth – it is soup after all).

Step 4. Then knit that loop on the left hand needle as if it was a regular stitch. When you count your stitches at the end of this row, you will have one extra.

Handy HINT

When you try and knit the picked up loop, it will feel tight. Don't worry; this is exactly as it should feel. If it's really difficult to pick up to knit it, try using your left index finger to 'roll' it towards you. This should loosen it enough to pick it up and knit it.

My 'soup and scoop' method may seem funny, but I find little memory tricks like this make knitting easier for a beginner, especially when you are learning so many new and interesting techniques all at once.

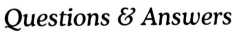

Questions & Answers

How do I increase in a purl row?

Exactly the same way. Remember 'soup and scoop.'

Zig-Zag Scarf

START KNITTING

Cast on 3 sts

Knit 1 row

1 K1, M1, K to end

Count 4 sts

2 Repeat this row until you have 25 sts

MAIN PATTERN

K2tog, K to end of row. (Count one less stitch.)

Repeat this row until you have 15 sts.

K1, M1, K to end of row. (Count one more stitch.)

Repeat this row until you have 25 sts.

3 Repeat from Main Pattern until your scarf is about 80 cm long (for child's size, or longer if it's for an adult).

FINISH ZIG-ZAG SCARF

To finish the scarf with a point (to match the beginning):

K2tog, K to end.

Repeat this row until you have one stitch left. Tie off (same as when you cast off).

Weave in all ends.

This is a twist on the simple scarf It is an excellent way to practice your increasing and decreasing.

By the time you've finished this scarf, you'll never forget how to increase (M1) and decrease (K2tog).

 Handy **HINT**

Rule Number One: don't forget to count your stitches at the end of every row! It is very important to keep the pattern looking even in this scarf.

1 Finding the bowl of soup can be harder with so few stitches on your knitting needle, but persevere, it is there

2 Repeat this row until you have 25 sts. Remember that you will be counting one more stitch every row

3 Your scarf is now starting zig-zag to take shape

YOU WILL NEED

100G ARAN YARN
(I always use a machine washable yarn for children's knitwear – I used
Debbie Bliss 'Cashmerino Aran' for this as it is soft but practical)

5MM KNITTING NEEDLES

Finishing Workshop

It is awful to have spent ages knitting something and have it spoilt in the end because the finishing isn't quite right.

You've already learnt how to sew up your pieces of knitting; here are a couple of techniques to add those final touches that will really boost the look and feel of your knitted garments.

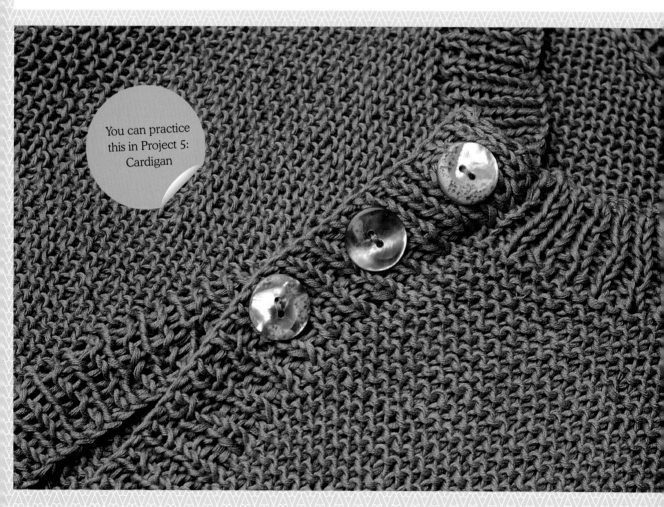

You can practice this in Project 5: Cardigan

Pick Up and Knit

Beginners often complain to me that the edges of their knitting don't look tidy. Pick-Up and Knit is a way of working a border onto your knitting to hide all untidy edges and give a instant professional finish. I love using it on my cardigans. Use 'pick up and knit' to add a rib border to your stocking stitch

knitting – it is pretty much the only way I know to stop your stocking stitch from curling up.

You'll need a crochet hook to pick up the stitches – use a size close to that of your knitting needles.

Step 1. Lay out your work so that the knitting needle is facing towards the left, and the right side of the work is facing up. You will be picking up the stitches from the right to the left of your knitting (this seems backwards to how you would usually work), and not from left to right as you might imagine it to be done.

Step 2. Insert the crochet hook into the edge of the work, making sure it slides under two loops of yarn. Face the hooked head of the crochet hook away from you. (The loose end of the yarn at the beginning of this section will be woven in to the back of the work to secure it).

Step 3. Wrap the yarn over the crochet hook going **over** and then **under** the hook, and use the crochet hook to pull that wrapped yarn through the same stitches you inserted the hook into. (Basically this means to pulling out the crochet hook; it will bring the yarn with it in a loop.)

Step 4. Place the pulled through loop of yarn onto the knitting needle.

Repeat this to the end of the Pick-up section. Your knitting pattern will tell you how many stitches to pick up.

The pattern will then ask you to knit a border before casting off.

Questions & Answers

How far apart should I be picking up each stitch?

This is hard to explain, but it will come with experience. You roughly pick up one stitch per row of the work. You know how far apart each stitch should look on your knitting needle so remember not to pick up stitches too close or far apart from each other. You don't need to worry too much as this is one of those magic techniques that almost always ends up looking great. Also, patterns may tell you how many stitches to pick up.

Eyelet Buttonholes

Learning how to knit buttonholes into your work can seem daunting, but it's a nifty trick to have up your sleeve – and the method I'm using couldn't be simpler. It'll work if you want to add a small button, for bigger buttonholes there are different methods you can learn at a later date.

I've shown the buttonholes on a piece of knitting that has been made with Pick-up and Knit and a 1x1 Rib; this is just as you will do it in the Cardigan pattern, which is the next project.

Start your rib pattern. Then on a right side row, start your buttonholes.

Knit every stitch on your buttonhole row (even if you are working in rib – don't worry, it'll look right in the end) until you get to where you want your buttonhole to sit. Then follow the instructions below.

1

2

3

Step 1. Bring your yarn to the front of your work (YF) as if you were about to purl.

Step 2. Then, instead of purling, knit two stitches together (K2tog). Repeat these steps every time you want a buttonhole until the end of the row. At this stage, it's very important to count your stitches at the end of your row to ensure you have the same number as when you started the row, otherwise your rib stitch won't work.

Step 3. Then continue the rest of your rows in your 1x1 rib pattern. The eyelet buttonholes will appear in the next row. Remember to cast off in rib with the wrong side of the work facing you (see the Stitch Patterns Workshop on p.48).

This method of making buttonholes works in the same way on the knit side of stocking stitch and either side of garter stitch.

Knitter's Notes

Remember to count the same number of stitches between each buttonhole, otherwise the buttons will look wonky when the garment is fastened. Plan button-placement before you start knitting the row. Of course, most patterns will tell you how many stitches to count between rows, so you won't need to worry.

Knitting two stitches together with the yarn in the front instead of the back gives you the same number of stitches at the end of your row, and also leaves you with a decorative hole – also used as a buttonhole.

You can practice
finishing with
Project 5: Cardigan

Cardigan (for a baby or child)

This is a pattern for a little cardigan that knits in one piece and is finished using Pick Up and Knit to give it an ultra professional look. If you are sick of cutsey pastel colours, why not try knitting this in bright, stimulating colours or stripes. Then you can have some fun choosing funky buttons as well! Also, as it's knitted in one piece, there's much less sewing (which I find the least fun part of knitting.)

Baby clothes need not be pastels!

Classic colours with funky buttons

This pattern includes instructions for two different sizes. Both sets of instructions are incorporated, so you have to remember whether you are knitting for a baby or a child, and follow the numbers accordingly. The numbers for the baby size will be written first, with the child size in brackets immediately after. It may be worth using a pencil to lightly circle all relevant numbers for the size you are knitting before you begin, so that it is clear which instructions you are following throughout.

Sizing: Baby = 3/6 months. Child = 2/3 years.

My sizes are approximate, as they will depend on your unpredictable beginner's tension. If in doubt, choose the bigger size – the child can always grow into it! Also, as you are using a bigger needle than is customary for double-knit yarn, your cardigan will be extra stretchy so it will be wearable by a growing child for longer. It is always better to go bigger with children's garments if you have any doubts at all about sizes.

Use the layout at the start of the pattern to help you get your bearings as you follow this pattern.

YOU WILL NEED

DOUBLE-KNIT YARN. 200G (250G)
(I like Sirdar 'Luxury Soft Cotton DK' which is machine washable – best for tiny sticky fingers. This is an extra long yarn so you need less than you would with most other double-knit yarns - but do shop around for cool yarns.)

5MM KNITTING NEEDLES

CROCHET HOOK FOR PICKING UP AND KNITTING

DARNING NEEDLE

3 SMALL (1 CM) BUTTONS

PATTERN LAYOUT

This is the shape of the piece you are knitting. You will start knitting from the back. Then it folds in half along the dashed line. The cardigan sews together along the underarms and sides.

KEY TO DIAGRAM

Fold lines

START KNITTING

FOLD LINE

FINISH KNITTING

ABBREVIATIONS:

K =Knit

P = Purl

St(s) = Stitch(es)

M1 = Make one stitch

YF = Yarn forward: bring yarn to the front of work

1x1 rib = Knit one stitch, purl one stitch, repeat this sequence to the end of the row

K2tog = Knit two stitches together

START KNITTING

BEGIN WITH THE BACK

Cast on 50 sts (56 sts)

TRANSLATION: Cast on 50 sts for the baby cardigan and 56 sts for the child size cardigan.

1 K1, P1, rib for 8 rows (this is the same for both sizes). Keeping a tally of the rows as you have knitted them will help you with this.

2 Garter stitch (knit every row) until your knitting measures 18cm (23cm) from the beginning.

NOW START THE SLEEVE SECTION OF THE CARDIGAN

3 Turn (swap the needles around in your hands as if to work the next row) and cast on 24 sts (45 sts) using the first stitch on the left needle as if it was the slipknot. This is the first sleeve.

Count 74 sts (101 sts)

Knit across row. Turn and cast on 24 sts (45 sts) for the second sleeve.

4 Count 98 sts (146 sts)

Knit until piece measures 10cm (11cm) from last cast-on edge.

NOW YOU WILL START CREATING THE SPACE FOR THE NECK OPENING OF THE CARDIGAN

5 K 39 sts (58 sts). You will be ignoring these stitches for the time being. Cast off 20 sts (30 sts) for back of neck. (TRANSLATION: K1, K1, cast off the first knitted stitch, K1, cast off, and so on...keep counting your casting off until you have 38 (57) sts on the left needle and 1 st on the right needle.)

6 Knit the remaining 38 sts (57 sts) on the left needle.

1 1x1 rib border

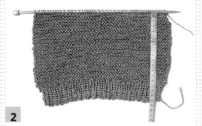

2 This is the back of the cardigan

3 Cast on for sleeve

4 Now you have cast on for both sleeves

5 Knit 39 (58 sts) then cast off 20 (30) sts for back of neck

6 Keep casting off until you have 38 (57) stitches on the left needle and 1 stitch on the right needle (ignoring the first 39 (58) stitches) knit the remaining 38 (57) stitches.

CONTINUED...

7 You will now be working on this side all the way to the end of the cardigan; then you will go back and work on the 39 sts (58 sts) sts on the other side, which you will ignore for now.

Knit the 39 sts (58 sts) for 4 rows (6 rows.)

Now increase your stitches one at a time – always on the neck side of the cardigan:

K until 1 st remains. M1, K1. Count 40 sts (59 sts).

K1, M1, k to end. Count 41 sts (60 sts).

K until 1 st remains. M1, K1.

There are now 42 sts (61 sts). COUNT!

8 Turn (swap the needles around in your hands as if to work the next row) and cast on 9 sts (12 sts).

Count 51 sts (73 sts).

Knit until sleeve measures 20cm (23cm) from the start of the sleeve section, (ending with the point of the needle facing the 'hand-hole' end of the work.)

9 Cast off 23 sts (45 sts) (make sure you are casting these off on the sleeve side and not the body side of the cardigan). Knit to end of row.

10 Count 28 sts (this is the same for both sizes of the cardigan).

Knit these 28 sts until piece measures 15cm (20cm) (ending with the point of the needle facing the front opening.)

K1, P1, rib for 8 rows.

11 Cast off in rib – remember that you've been working in rib, so you must cast off in rib. See: Stitch Patterns (p.48). Always cast off with wrong side of the work facing you.

OTHER SIDE: LEFT

12 Join yarn to sts at neck end: pull the end of yarn from the ball underneath the first stitch on the knitting needle and tie it into a knot with itself. You can weave the end in later.

You will now be working on the 39 sts (58 sts) that you have been ignoring up to this point.

Knit across these 39 sts (58 sts) for 4 rows (6 rows).

K1, M1, knit to end. Count 40 sts (59 sts).

K to last st, M1, K1. Count 41 sts (60 sts).

K1, M1, knit to end.

There are now 42 sts (61 sts). Count!

Knit 1 row.

Turn (swap the needles around in your hands to work the next row).

7

You will now work on the first 39 (58) stitches to the end of the cardigan, ignoring the other 39 (58) stitches.

8

Cast on for the front of the neck

9a

Cast off 23 (45) stitches for the sleeve

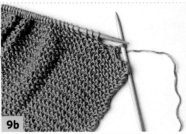

9b

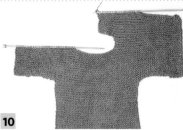

10

You will now work this side of the cardigan to the end, then go back to complete the other side

11

Now you will go back to the 39 sts (58 sts) you have been ignoring and finish knitting the other side of the cardigan

12a

Use a crochet hook to attach the new yarn

12b

Secure the new yarn with a knot

CONTINUED...

Cast on 9 sts (12 sts) – ensure this is on neck edge).

Count 51 sts (73 sts).

Knit until sleeve measures 20cm (23cm) making sure the needle is facing the 'hand-hole' end after the last row.

Cast off 23 sts (45 sts) from the hand side of the sleeve. Knit to end of row.

Count 28 sts (same for both sizes).

Knit these 28 sts until piece measures 15cm (20cm) – ending with the point of the needle facing away from the front opening.

K1, P1, rib for 8 rows.

13 Cast off in rib.

NECK BAND

14 Lay out the cardigan with the right side facing up, pick up and knit evenly across right front, back and left front of cardigan. Always pick up an even number of stitches. (For instructions, see 13. Finishing Workshop on p.62.)

K1, P1, rib for 8 rows.

Cast off in 1x1 rib. Always cast off on the wrong side of the work.

Now you will knit the front bands of the cardigan:

RIGHT FRONT – BUTTON SIDE

15 With the right side of the work facing you, pick up and knit evenly across right front opening – start at the bottom of the front opening, and pick up all the way to the top of the neck band. Always pick up an even number of stitches. It's a good idea to make a note of the number of stitches you pick up on the right front so that you can pick up the same number on the left front.

K1, P1, rib for 8 rows.

Cast off in 1x1 rib.

LEFT FRONT – BUTTONHOLE SIDE

With the right side of the work facing you, pick up and knit evenly across right front. Always pick up an even number of stitches – try to pick up the same number of stitches as you did on the right front. This time you start at the top of the neck band and work your way down to the bottom of the left front opening.

K1, P1, rib for 3 rows.

Buttonhole row: (Knit 5 sts, yf k2tog), repeat the bracket sequence twice more (a total of three times for three buttonholes), knit to end of row. See: Eyelet buttonholes (p.64) for further instructions.

16 K1, P1 rib for four rows. Your three buttonholes should appear after the first of these four rib rows.

Cast off in 1x1 rib.

Securely stitch the three buttons into position, so they match up with the buttonholes.

Now to sew the cardigan up. As you have knitted the cardigan in one piece, there is a minimal amount of sewing to be done...hooray!

Fold the cardigan in half along the middle – see the Layout diagram (p.68). Be sure to line up the underneath of the sleeves and the sides of the body exactly. You can sew up using backstitch, or using garter mattress stitch along the side of the body, and backstitch on the underneath of the sleeves (remember to hold the knitting right-side out when using mattress stitch, and inside out when using backstitch).

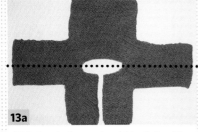

13a

This is what you should be left with. The dotted line is the fold line.

13b

Your cardigan is really starting to take shape: now for the finishing!

14a

Lay work with right side facing up and pick up and knit starting from the right front

14b

Use crochet hook to pick up and knit the collar

14c

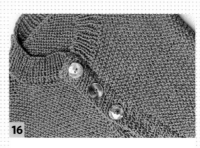

14d

Pick up an even number of stitches around the whole collar

14e

This is what the neck band should look like when you have finished picking up and knitting; you are about to start knitting the 1x1 rib neck band.

15

Now you will knit the button bands

16

Button bands

Flower

This is one of my favourite patterns in the book; it's so easy, and lends itself to infinite lovely variations.

Use your knitted flowers in different ways

You can use any yarn, any needles, any colour. Each different yarn you use will give you a different sized flower (from the same pattern). You can layer the flowers on top of each other to make an elaborate corsage. Sew a pin in the back to turn it into a brooch. Or attach a clip to wear it as a hairpin. Making these gorgeous flowers is a great excuse to use some of the crazy novelty yarns available. I love to sew the flowers to some of the other projects as a decoration. What about a baby cardigan with some mini flowers firmly attached? Or the girly scarf with a flower brooch? The options are endless! Go on – use your imagination and be creative!

YOU WILL NEED

YARN
any that you've got lying around (go wild!)

KNITTING NEEDLES
any that fit the yarn

DARNING NEEDLE

The pattern will give you a different flower depending on the yarn you use

ABBREVIATIONS:

K = Knit

K2tog = Knit two stitches together

START KNITTING

1 Cast on 20 sts.

2 Knit 5 rows.

3 K2tog, repeat to end of row.

4 Count 10 sts.

FINISH

5 Drawstring finish: Cut yarn leaving a long end. Thread this onto a darning needle. Pass the stitches from the knitting needle onto the darning needle. (See Knit Hats on p.52 for further instructions about the drawstring finish).

6 Pull tight (you should see the flower shape start to emerge) and sew up seam. Weave in all ends.

1

Cast on 20 sts.

2

Knit 5 rows.

3

K2tog, repeat to end of row.

4

Count 10 sts.

5

Drawstring finish: Cut yarn leaving a long end. Thread this onto a darning needle. Pass the stitches from the knitting needle onto the darning needle. (See Knit Hats on p.52 for further instructions about the drawstring finish).

6a

Pull tight (you should now see the flower shape start to emerge) and sew up seam.

6b

Weave in all ends.

Now go crazy with your imagination – knitted flowers everywhere!

Cable Stitches Workshop

A cable is a pattern in knitting that looks like a twisted section against a plain background.

Once you learn how to create a basic twist, you can experiment and knit all sorts of beautiful patterns. In this section you will learn how to make a simple forward cable and back cable against a garter stitch background.

For cable knitting you will need a cable needle - a small knitting needle with a 'V' or 'U' shaped bend in it. This is used to transfer and hold stitches so they can be knitted in different orders.

Forward and back cable stitch

Cable Stitches

I suggest you make a small practice square using the instructions in this workshop before moving on to the next project, which shows you how to knit a cable bag.

Cast on 30 sts (to make a practice piece). You will be repeating a four-row pattern to create this cable practice square.

Row 1: K6, P6, K6, P6, K6.
Row 2: K 1 row.
Row 3: K6, P6, K6, P6, K6.

The first three rows in the cabling pattern are quite simple to understand. Remember to bring the yarn forward and back between the knit and purl stitches and remember to count at the end of every row! There's no escaping from Rule Number One.

Then we get to the interesting bit. This is the row where the cable twist is added:

CF = Cable Forward.
CB = Cable Back.
Row 4: K6, CF6, K6, CB6, K6.

CF6 means that six stitches will be used to make the twist. F means that the first three stitches will be in front of the second three stitches. (And vice versa with the CB).

To work the cable row – Row 4:

Step 1. Knit six stitches.

Step 2. CF6: Pass the next three stitches onto the cable needle – you don't knit these stitches, you simply slip them over from the main needle to the cable needle.

Step 3. Hold this to the front of your knitting (towards your body). Knit the next three stitches (they may feel a little tight).

Step 4. Slip the first three stitches from the cable needle back onto the left hand needle.

Step 5. Knit these three stitches, (they may feel a little tight). Knit six stitches.

Step 6. CB6: Put the next three stitches onto the cable needle. Hold this to the back of your knitting

Knit the next three stitches (they may feel a little tight).

Slip the first three stitches from the cable needle back onto the left-hand needle.

Knit these three stitches.

Knit six stitches.

This row will put the twist into the stitches to create the cable pattern. The next three rows will put enough space between the cable rows to show off the pattern.

You can practice cable stitches with Project 7: Cable Project Bag (p.81)

Step 7. Repeat the four-row pattern until you have a square (or feel that you have practiced enough).

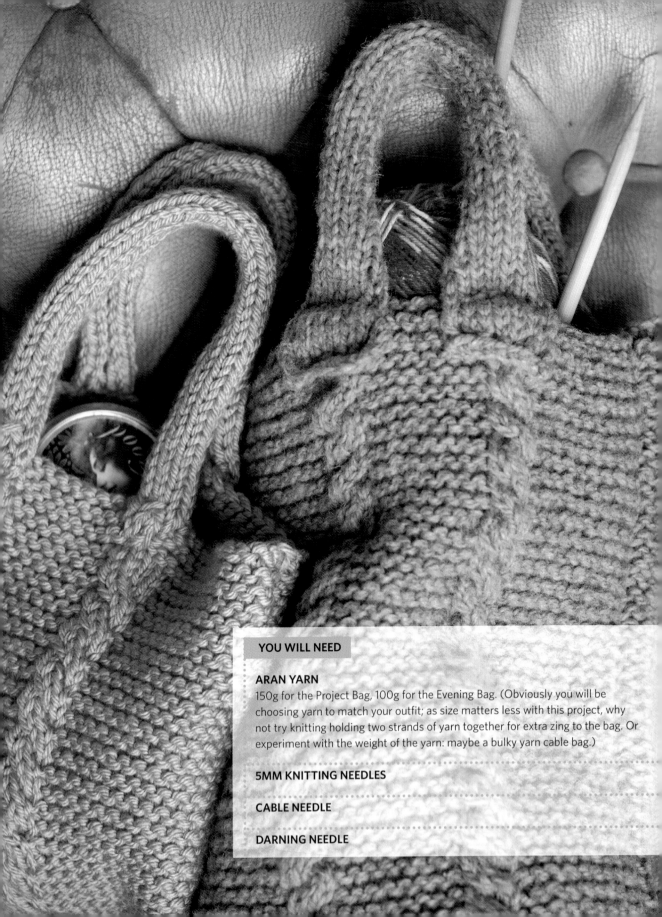

YOU WILL NEED

ARAN YARN
150g for the Project Bag, 100g for the Evening Bag. (Obviously you will be choosing yarn to match your outfit; as size matters less with this project, why not try knitting holding two strands of yarn together for extra zing to the bag. Or experiment with the weight of the yarn: maybe a bulky yarn cable bag.)

5MM KNITTING NEEDLES

CABLE NEEDLE

DARNING NEEDLE

Cable Project Bag

ABBREVIATIONS:

St(s) = Stitch(es)	
K = Knit	
P = Purl	
CF = Cable forward	
CB = Cable back	

START KNITTING

HANDLES (MAKE 2)

Cast on 8 sts

Stocking stitch until handle measures 25cm

Cast off

BAG

Cast on 40 sts

K 1 row

K12, P4, K8, P4, K12.

K 1 row

K12, P4, K8, P4, K12

K12, CF4, K8, CB4, K12

Repeat the last four rows until the piece measures 60cm for the Project Bag, (30cm for the Evening Bag.)

To finish: K12, P4, K8, P4, K12

K 1 row

K12, P4, K8, P4, K12

1 Cast off. Fold the piece in half (right side facing out) and sew up along the long sides using garter mattress stitch. Weave in all ends.

2 Attach the handles firmly - I used an X-shaped stitch - very pretty as well as secure.

My students are always asking me where they can get a good knitting bag - I think that a knitting bag is a useful thing to have if you want to carry projects around, but in my experience, your yarn stash will soon grow so large that you will need something more the size of a suitcase if you want to store everything in one bag! Instead of trying to design a bizarre knitted suitcase, this pattern will help you create your very own Cable Project Bag. Roomy enough to accommodate your current work in progress, it will be an essential piece of kit for holding yarn, needles, patterns and other gadgets so that you can carry your knitting with you wherever you go.

This bag incorporates a simple cable stitch that is easy to knit and exciting enough to impress all your friends! It can be knitted in a variety of sizes and used as a knitting bag, or for books and papers, or even as a little evening bag if you make it smaller.

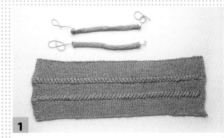

1 Layout of Cable Project Bag and handles

2 Sew handles on securely

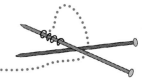

Lacy Wrap

This versatile wrap is a beguilingly simple way to create a gorgeous lacy knit.

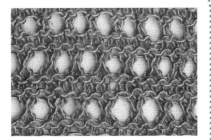

Garter eyelet stitch

Using a double-knit yarn, you can choose something utterly luxurious like silk yarn to add glamour to this shawl. It can be worn in a variety of ways, and it is the perfect way to ward off chills on a spring evening. This pattern is also a terrific challenge to the ambitious beginner knitter. You will notice that the needle size I am using is bigger than the size recommended for double-knit yarn; this is because I want to give your shawl an open lacy weave which will make it a beautiful flowing piece of fabric.

YOU WILL NEED

150G DOUBLE-KNIT YARN
(you can choose from the huge variety of double-knit yarns available; I used Debbie Bliss Pure Silk for my wrap – simply lovely silk yarn, and extra long so you would only need two skeins. Debbie Bliss Alpaca Silk DK is a good choice for a bit more warmth – 3 skeins needed in this yarn).

6MM KNITTING NEEDLES

Handy HINT

Practice makes perfect. To knit a garter eyelet practice square:

• Cast on 21 sts

• Knit 3 rows

• K1 (yf, k2tog) repeat bracketed section to the end of the row

• Knit 4 rows

• Repeat the last 5 rows until you have knitted a practice square.

ABBREVIATIONS:

K = Knit

St(s) = Stitch(es)

YF = Yarn forward: bring your yarn to the front of your knitting over the top of the needles (see Workshop: Stitch Patterns, p.48)

M1 = Make one stitch (see Workshop: Increasing, p.58)

K2tog = Knit two stitches together

START KNITTING

Cast on 4sts

Row 1: K 1 row. Count 4sts.

1 Row 2: K1, M1, K until you have 1 stitch left on your left needle. M1, K1. Count 6sts. (Finding where to M1 will be tricky with so few stitches, but persevere as it will become easier the more you knit.)

Row 3: K 1 row. Count 6sts.

2 Row 4 – Eyelet row: K1, M1, (YF, K2tog), repeat the bracketed section until 1 stitch remains on the left needle. M1, K1. Count 8 sts. (The stitches will look uneven after this row but will all straighten out after Row 5.)

Row 5: K 1 row. Count 8sts.

3 Repeat these 5 rows until you count 114sts.

Cast off loosely. When casting off, if you are worried that your cast off is too tight, try casting off using a 7mm needle. This will make the cast off looser.

Weave in your ends.

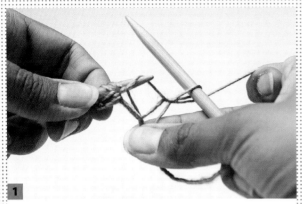

1 Make one stitch

2a Yarn forward

2b Knit two stitches together

3 Your knitting may look untidy at the start, but persevere and you will see the pretty eyelet pattern emerge once you have repeated the pattern a few times

I find the following chart helpful for keeping track of where I am with this pattern. I just cross off the numbers at the end of each row.

ROW	STITCH COUNT													
1	4	8	12	16	20	24	28	32	36	40	44	48	52	56
2 INC	6	10	14	18	22	26	30	34	38	42	46	50	54	58
3	6	10	14	18	22	26	30	34	38	42	46	50	54	58
4 EYELET INC	8	12	16	20	24	28	32	36	40	44	48	52	56	60
5	8	12	16	20	24	28	32	36	40	44	48	52	56	60

ROW	STITCH COUNT													
1	60	64	68	72	76	80	84	88	92	96	100	104	108	112
2 INC	62	66	70	74	78	82	86	90	94	98	102	106	110	114
3	62	66	70	74	78	82	86	90	94	98	102	106	110	
4 EYELET INC	64	68	72	76	80	84	88	92	96	100	104	108	112	
5	64	68	72	76	80	84	88	92	96	100	104	108	112	

Mittens

This is a pattern for a simple, stylish pair of mittens. Knitted in aran yarn (a slightly heavier weight than double-knit), these are warm, fun and quick to make! What more could you ask for in mittens? Also, this pattern provides a real knitting challenge that you will definitely be ready for if you have followed the book this far.

There are three sizes to choose from: Baby Mittens, Child Mittens and the quintessential Lady Mittens. The Baby Mittens pattern is written separately as it is different to the patterns for children's and women's sizes.

Child and Lady Mittens

Any aran-weight yarn will work wonderfully for this pattern. Aran yarn is slightly thicker than double-knit, and knitting it up on 5mm knitting needles will give you a very warm, cosy pair of mittens.

Unlike most mitten and glove patterns, my mitts fit either hand so you can sidestep that annoying mistake everyone seems to do when they first knit mittens - making two mittens for one hand! (It happens to the best of us.) Just make two the same and forget all about left or right or nasty 'reverse shaping.' Don't worry if they look a bit small as you are knitting them, they are meant to fit snugly, and they will have enough stretch to be comfortable.

YOU WILL NEED

CHILD'S MITTENS

50G ARAN-WEIGHT YARN

5MM KNITTING NEEDLES

DARNING NEEDLE

LADIES' MITTENS

100G ARAN-WEIGHT YARN
(I used Debbie Bliss Cashmerino yarn for my pair and they turned out soft and extra warm!)

5MM KNITTING NEEDLES

DARNING NEEDLE

ABBREVIATIONS:

K = Knit

P = Purl

St st = Stocking stitch

St(s) = Stitch(es)

1 x 1 rib = Knit one stitch, purl one stitch

M1 = Make one stitch (See Workshop: Increasing)

K2tog = Knit two stitches together

START KNITTING

Cast on 20 sts. Try to make the cast-on stitches looser than you usually might.

1 1 x 1 rib for 10 rows.

START INCREASING FOR THUMB

2 K10, M1, K10. Count 21sts.

P 1 row.

K10, M1, K1, M1, K10. Count 23sts.

P 1 row.

K 1 row.

P 1 row.

K10, M1, K3, M1, K10. Count 25sts.

P 1 row.

K 1 row.

P 1 row.

K10, M1, K5, M1, K10. Count 27sts.

P 1 row.

K 1 row.

P 1 row.

CHILD'S MITTENS

Follow the right-hand page for instructions for Child's Mittens. Please note that the text on the images corresponds with the child-size mittens, but the images will be a useful aid when knitting either size.

Handy HINT

If you are having trouble making your cast-on stitches looser, try casting on with a knitting needle 1mm bigger than that you'll use for the rest of the pattern. Then knit your first row onto the recommended needle size for the pattern (discarding the larger needle), and continue following the pattern with the recommended needles.

1

1 x 1 rib for 10 rows.

Follow the left hand page for
instructions on ladies mittens

ABBREVIATIONS:

K = Knit

P = Purl

St st = Stocking stitch

St(s) = Stitch(es)

1 x 1 rib = Knit one stitch, purl one stitch

M1 = Make one stitch (See Workshop: Increasing)

K2tog = Knit two stitches together

START KNITTING

Cast on 24 sts. Try to make the cast-on stitches looser than you usually might.

1 1 x 1 rib for 15 rows.

START INCREASING FOR THUMB

2 K12, M1, K12. Count 25sts.

P 1 row.

K12, M1, K1, M1, K12. Count 27sts.

P 1 row.

K 1 row.

P 1 row.

K12, M1, K3, M1, K12. Count 29sts.

P 1 row.

K 1 row.

P 1 row.

K12, M1, K5, M1, K12. Count 31sts.

P 1 row.

K 1 row.

P 1 row

2

K10, M1, K10. Count 21sts.

CONTINUE...

CHILD'S MITTENS CONTINUED....

K10, M1, K7, M1, K10. Count 29sts.

P 1 row.

K 1 row.

P 1 row.

K10, M1, K9, M1, K10. Count 31sts.

P 1 row.

K 1 row.

P 1 row.

3 SEPARATE FOR THUMB

K 20sts. Turn – this means swap the knitting needles around in your hands as if you were about to start knitting the next row. The reason for this is that you are about to knit the thumb to completion before working on the main finger-section of the mitten.

P 9. Turn.

K 9. Turn.

4

Continuing to 'turn' in this manner, working on these centre 9sts only, stocking stitch until the thumb section measures 6cm from separation, making sure that the last row you do is a purl row. At this stage, it's a good idea to count your rows as you work them so that you can ensure both hands are the same size.

DECREASE FOR THE TOP OF THE THUMB

(K1, K2tog), repeat 3 times in total. Count 6sts.

P 1 row.

(K1, K2tog), repeat 2 times in total. Count 4sts.

P 1 row.

3

Separate for thumb

5

Drawstring finish for thumb

5 DRAWSTRING FINISH FOR TOP OF THUMB:

Cut the yarn leaving a long end. Thread this end onto a darning needle. Transfer the 4 stitches from the knitting needle onto the darning needle one by one and pull tight.

6

Fold thumb in half and sew up from the top of the thumb to the base of the thumb. Remember: inside-out if you are using backstitch (as I did) or right-side out if you are using mattress stitch. See Workshop: Sewing Up.

4

Work on thumb only

6

Sew up thumb

LADIES' MITTENS CONTINUED....

K12, M1, K7, M1, K12. Count 33sts.

P 1 row.

K 1 row.

P 1 row.

K12, M1, K9, M1, K12. Count 35sts.

P 1 row.

K 1 row.

P 1 row.

K12, M1, K11, M1, K12. Count 37sts.

3 **SEPARATE FOR THUMB**
P 24sts. Turn – this means swap the knitting
needles around in your hands as if you were
about to start knitting the next row. The reason
for this is that you are about to knit the thumb
to completion before working on the main
finger-section of the mitten.

K 11. Turn.

P 11. Turn.

4 Continuing to 'turn' in this manner, working on
these centre 11sts only, stocking stitch until the
thumb section measures 6cm from separation,
making sure that the last row you do is a purl
row. At this stage, it is a good idea to count your
rows as you work them so that you can ensure
both hands are the same size.

DECREASE FOR THE TOP OF THE THUMB
(K1, K2tog), repeat bracketed section 3 times
in total, K2. Count 8 sts.

P 1 row.

(K1, K2tog), repeat twice, K2. Count 6 sts.

P 1 row.

(K1, K2tog), repeat twice. Count 4 sts.

5 **DRAWSTRING FINISH FOR TOP OF THUMB**
Cut the yarn leaving a long end (about 80cm).
Thread this end onto a darning needle. Transfer
the 4sts from the knitting needle onto the
darning needle one by one and pull tight.

6 Fold thumb in half and sew up from the top of the
thumb to the base of the thumb. See Step 6
opposite.

CONTINUE...

CHILD'S MITTENS CONTINUED....

Turn the thumb right-side out.

7 Using the remainder of the long end of the yarn you used to sew up the thumb, and with right side (the knit side) of the work facing you, M1, then knit 11 sts. (With this M1, it's not as easy to find the loop to pick up between the stitches – just persevere). Count 23sts.

Purl 1 row.

At some point soon you will have to join new yarn – in the same way that you would normally.

Starting with a knit row, stocking stitch these 23sts until the work measures 6cm from the base of the thumb, making sure that the last row you do is a purl row. At this stage, it's a good idea to count your rows as you work them so that you can ensure both hands are the same size.

DECREASE FOR TOP OF MITTEN:

(K1, K2tog) a total of 7 times, K2. Count 16 sts.

P 1 row.

(K1, K2tog) a total of 5 times, K1. Count 11 sts

P 1 row.

8 **DRAWSTRING FINISH FOR TOP OF MITTEN**
Cut the yarn, leaving a long end. Thread this end onto a darning needle. Transfer the remaining 11sts from the knitting needle onto the darning needle one by one and pull tight.

9 Fold the mitten in half and sew it up all down the side.

Weave in all your ends.

7
Use the remainder of the long end of the yarn

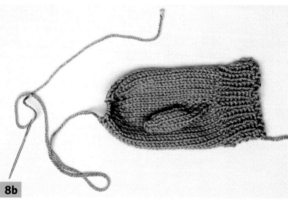

8b
Cut the yarn leaving a long end.

Knit another the same!

8a

Drawstring finish for top of mitten

9

Fold the mitten in half and sew it up all down the side

Turn the thumb right-side out.

7   Using the remainder of the long end of the yarn you used to sew up the thumb, and with right side (the knit side) of the work facing you, M1, then knit 13 sts. Count 27sts. (With this M1, it's not as easy to find the loop to pick up between the stitches – just persevere).

Purl 1 row.

(At some point soon you will have to join new yarn – in the same way that you would normally).

Starting with a knit row, stocking stitch these 27 sts until the work measures 11cm from the base of the thumb, making sure that the last row you do is a purl row. At this stage, it's a good idea to count your rows as you work them so that you can ensure both hands are the same size.

DECREASE FOR THE TOP OF THE MITTEN:

(K1, K2tog), repeat a total of 9 times.
Count 18sts.

P 1 row.

(K1, K2tog), repeat 6 times in total. Count 12sts.

P 1 row.

(K1, K2tog), repeat 4 times in total. Count 8sts.

P 1 row

8   **DRAWSTRING FINISH FOR TOP OF MITTEN**
Cut the yarn leaving a long end. Thread this end onto a darning needle. Transfer the eight stitches from the knitting needle onto the darning needle one by one and pull tight.

9   Fold the mitten in half and sew it up all down the side. Weave in all your ends.

Wear with warmth!

Baby 'Hand-Hat' Mittens

When knitting these baby mittens, you will notice that they have no thumbs. Don't worry, it's not a mistake – there's a good reason for the thumb-free mitten. All the mummies, daddies and baby-sitters amongst you will know that small babies often scratch their faces as they are waving their little hands about. Mittens with thumbs aren't practical in such a tiny size, but these little 'hand-hats' are perfect to protect delicate soft skin.

They are as quick to knit as baby booties, and make an unusual, thoughtful and practical gift for any new baby.

Please note that these are not knitted in the same Aran-weight yarn as the child and adult mittens. Any double knit will do for this pattern, but you should consider a 100% cotton if you are concerned about baby allergies.

YOU WILL NEED

BABY MITTENS

50G DOUBLE KNIT YARN
(this will give you plenty of yarn for a pair of matching booties too). I prefer to choose natural cotton yarns as the mitts are likely to end up in baby-mouths: Sirdar 'Luxury Soft Cotton DK' is a good choice. Cotton yarns spilt easily so be extra careful when knitting or you'll end up with extra stitches.)

4MM KNITTING NEEDLES

DARNING NEEDLE

ABBREVIATIONS:

K = Knit	
P = Purl	
St(s) = Stitch(es)	
K2tog = Knit two stitches together	

START KNITTING

Cast on 24sts

1 K1, P1, rib for 8 rows

2 Garter stitch (knit every row) until your knitting measures 7cm from the beginning.

3 START DECREASING FOR MITTEN-TOP:

(K1, K2tog.) Repeat the bracketed sequence 8 times. Count 16sts.

K 1 row.

(K1, K2tog.) Repeat 5 times. K1. Count 11sts.

K 1 row.

(K1, K2tog.) Repeat 3 times. K2. Count 8sts.

K 1 row.

4 DRAWSTRING FINISH FOR TOP OF MITT:

Cut the yarn leaving a long end. Thread this end onto a darning needle. Transfer the 8sts from the knitting needle onto the darning needle one by one and pull tight.

Fold the mitt in half and sew up.

5 Weave in all your ends. Make another exactly the same and...ahh! Tiny baby mittens.

1

K1, P1, rib for 8 rows

2

Garter stitch (knit every row) until your knitting measures 7cm from the beginning

3

Decrease to eight stitches

4

Drawstring finish for top of mitt

5

Fold the mitt in half and sew up.

Hot Water Bottle Cover

This is the ultimate in cosy winter gifts – give it to your Mum for Christmas, your Granny for her birthday, or keep it for yourself. Your toes need never be cold again!

Any double-knit yarn will work in this pattern; just remember that you will be taking this knitting to bed with you so choose something extra soft.

A mixture of moss stitch and stocking stitch makes this one-piece knit both pretty and simple. If you need a refresher on your moss stitch, go to the chapter about stitch patterns and knit a practice square – a little bit of practice goes a long way in knitting.

YOU WILL NEED

100G DOUBLE-KNIT YARN
Something suitable for cuddling up to, but still beautiful – there are endless choices in DK yarn.

4MM NEEDLES

DARNING NEEDLE

7 SMALL FLAT BUTTONS (1 CM)

SEWING NEEDLE AND THREAD FOR BUTTONS

PATTERN LAYOUT

This is the shape of the piece you will be knitting. The hot water bottle cover is knitted in one piece and folded in the middle and sewn.

KEY TO DIAGRAM

Fold lines ·······························
Buttons ⊕ ⊕ ⊕ ⊕ ⊕ ⊕ ⊕

START KNITTING HERE:
← Cast on 41sts
  Moss stitch 7cm

FOLD ···

← Stocking stitch to 30cm from the beginning

← Cast off 12, K to end
  Cast off 12, P to end

← Moss stitch for 18cm

FOLD ···

← Cast on 12, K 1 row
  Cast on 12, P 1 row

← Stocking stitch for 30cm

← Moss stitch 10 rows
← Button hole row
← Moss st 8 rows

Cast off
END KNITTING

ABBREVIATIONS:

K = Knit	
P = Purl	
St(s) = Stitch(es)	
St st = Stocking stitch	
YF = Yarn forward	
K2tog = Knit two stitches together	
Rep = Repeat	

START KNITTING

Cast on 41sts

K1, P1, rep to end.
(Repeating this row with an odd number of stitches will create moss stitch.)

Moss stitch until piece measures 7cm from the beginning.

K 1 row
P 1 row
This is stocking stitch (st st).
Continue in st st until the entire piece measures 30cm from the beginning – making sure that the last row you do is a purl row (wrong side).

Cast off 12 sts, K to end. Count 29sts.
Cast off 12 sts, P to end. Count 17sts.

Moss stitch for 18 cm from cast off edge - making sure that the last row you do is on the wrong side of the work (purl stitch).

With the knitting in your left hand and the empty needle in your right - using the first stitch on the left needle as if it were the slipknot - cast on 12sts. Count 29sts.

K 1 row.
Turn (swap the needles in your hands). Cast on 12sts. Count 41sts.
P 1 row.

Buttonholes

Starting with a K row, stocking stitch until the piece from your new cast-on edge measures 30cm – making sure that the last row you do is a purl row (wrong side).

Moss stitch 10 rows.

BUTTONHOLE ROW:
K4, (yf, K2tog, K3), repeat the bracketed section until you have 5 sts left. K5.

Moss stitch 8 rows. (Your buttonholes will appear after the first of these 8 rows of moss stitch.)

Cast off.

SEWING UP:

Using darning needles and yarn, fold in half along the middle of the short moss stitch section (see Layout diagram). Sew up into hot water bottle shape, leaving flap at bottom.

Sew on seven small flat buttons in a matching sewing thread, using a normal sewing needle (the yarn and darning needle will probably be too thick to sew the buttons on with).

You will be left with a 7-cm flap with buttonholes to fold over and button so that your hot water bottle doesn't fall out of its cosy cover.

Buttons

Colinette hand-painted 'Cadenza' yarn was used for this cover

Necktie

It's pretty difficult to think up good gifts for my Dad every year.
He has a huge number of framed photos of me, fancy colognes
he never uses and shirts in all styles and colours!

So how about something any Big-Daddy won't be able to resist wearing?
I've designed a funky yet utterly wearable necktie that will appeal to his
inner Daddy-Cool! Why not make one for each of the men in your
family? Or wear your tie in the same way one stylish girl-knitter I know
does – it looks great on a high powered businesswoman with a pencil
skirt, crisp white shirt and a pair of sexy–librarian spectacles!

The tie is knitted in a fine 4-ply yarn that will not be too bulky for a tie,
but will still hold its shape well. Four-ply yarn is available in a variety of
materials and colours, but I've been using self-striping sock yarn; it
changes colour as if by magic and saves you having to weave in any
ends (and it's pretty exciting not knowing what colour will come next!).
You will notice that the tie is knitted entirely in garter stitch so that it lies
perfectly flat and makes a good tidy knot.

YOU WILL NEED

50G 4-PLY YARN
Self-striping sock yarn is a good choice for this knitted tie. Try Opal, Regia
or Schoeller and Stahl yarn. If you want a one-colour tie, any 4-ply yarn
will work.

2.75MM KNITTING NEEDLES

ABBREVIATIONS:

K = Knit

St(s) = Stitch(es)

M1 = Make one stitch

K2tog = Knit two stitches together

START KNITTING

Cast on 3sts

K 1 row.

1 K1, M1, K1, M1, K1. Count 5sts.

K 1 row.

K1, M1, knit until 1sts remains on left needle, M1, K1. Count 7sts.

You will find that the 'make one' is a bit difficult with so few stitches, but persevere - it will be worth it in the end.

2 You will see the 'V'-point of the tie emerging in your knitting. The first few M1s will feel a bit hard to find, but it will get easier the more rows you knit

Repeat the last two rows until you have 25sts.

K 5 rows

Decrease row: K1, K2tog, K until you have 3sts left, K2tog, K1. Count 23sts.

K 25 rows

Decrease row: K1, K2tog, K until you have 3sts left, K2tog, K1. Count 21sts.

K 25 rowsDecrease row: K1, K2tog, K until you have 3sts left, K2tog, K1. Count 19sts.

K 25 rows

Decrease row: K1, K2tog, K until you have 3sts left, K2tog, K1. Count 17sts.

K 25 rows

Decrease row: K1, K2tog, K until you have 3sts left, K2tog, K1. Count 15sts.

K 25 rows

Decrease row: K1, K2tog, K until you have 3sts left, K2tog, K1. Count 13sts.

K 25 rows

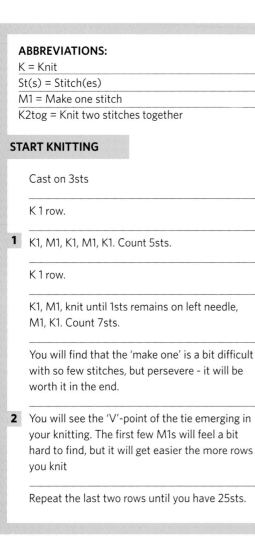

1 M1 = Make one stitch

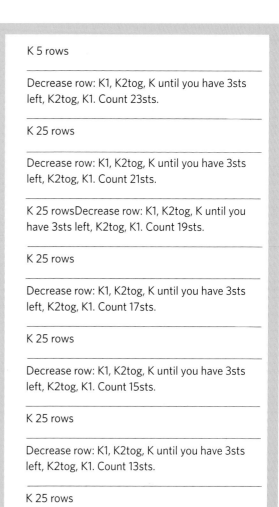

2 'V' of tie

Stylish ladies can wear this tie too!

Decrease row: K1, K2tog, K until you have 3sts left, K2tog, K1. Count 11sts.

Knit every row until the tie measures 140cm from the beginning.

Cast off

Weave in the ends at the beginning and end of the tie.

I like a Windsor knot myself!

Fingerless Wrist-Warmers

These wrist warmers are perfect for the funky teenager who wants an extra layer, or a sophisticated alternative to gloves for the discerning lady.

You can have some fun with them by sewing on accessories – try buttons, beads, knitted flowers or pom-poms. Try changing the yarn (or using self-striping) to make striped warmers, or play with the length on the wrist before starting the hand increase to turn them into slip-on sleeves... There are lots of options here for personalising and using your creativity. In no time at all you will have something funky, fun and original!

The main stitch used in this pattern is stocking stitch, and I've used an 'eyelet' pattern to create decorative holes. This is the same method you used when making buttonholes, but purely for prettiness without the need for buttons.

I know I'm only giving you a one-size-fits all option, but I've tried these on a variety of women's hands from skinny teenagers to curvaceous kittens – they will fit!

YOU WILL NEED

DOUBLE-KNIT YARN 100G
Be bold and brave with funky colours for cool teenagers – double-knit yarn comes in endless varieties

4MM KNITTING NEEDLES

DARNING NEEDLE

ABBREVIATIONS:

K = Knit

P = Purl

St(s) = Stitch(es)

K2tog = Knit two stitches together

YF = Bring the yarn to the front between the two needles

START KNITTING

Cast on 30sts loosely

K 1 row

P 1 row

K 1 row

P 1 row

Row 1: K14, yf , K2tog, K 14.

Row 2: P 1 row

Row 3: K 1 row

Row 4: P 1 row

Repeat the last four rows a further eight times each. You will count a total of nine eyelets when you are done.

START INCREASING FOR HAND:

K 13, yf, K3, yf, K14. Count 32sts.

P 1 row

K 1 row

P 1 row

K 13, yf, K5, yf, K14. Count 34sts.

P 1 row

K 1 row

P 1 row

K 13, yf, K7, yf, K14. Count 36sts.

Layout of wrist-warmers

Knitter's Notes

YF = Yarn forward. This is the same move you make when you bring the yarn to the front of the work, over the top of your knitting needles, when you are about to purl. But instead of purling, you knit two stitches together. K2tog with the yarn in front creates a decorative 'eyelet' pattern, whilst keeping the same number of stitches that you started with.

Handy HINT

Try and keep your cast-on stitches loose. If you have trouble with this, I suggest using a 5mm knitting needle to cast on with, then starting and continuing the knitting with 4mm needles for the rest of the pattern.

Handy HINT

When doing an eyelet pattern, it's especially important to count your stitches at the end of each row so that you have the correct number and your eyelet pattern is evenly distributed.

P 1 row

K 1 row

P 1 row

K 13, yf, K9, yf, K14. Count 38sts.

P 1 row

K 1 row

P 1 row

K 13, yf, K11, yf, K14. Count 40sts.

P 1 row

K 1 row

P 1 row

K 13, yf, K13, yf, K14. Count 42sts.

P 1 row

K 1 row

P 1 row

K 13, yf, K15, yf, K14. Count 44sts.

P 1 row

K 1 row

P 1 row

K 13, yf, K17, yf, K14. Count 46sts.

P 1 row

K 1 row

P 1 row

K 13, yf, K19, yf, K14. Count 48sts.

Questions & Answers

How am I increasing without a M1?
When you knit a stitch with the yarn forward, you create an increase and eyelet at the same time.

Sew up side seam using stocking mattress stitch.
See: Sewing Up Workshop on p.39

Sew up for thumb opening

P 1 row

K 1 row

P 1 row

K 1 row

Cast off leaving a long end for sewing (about 50cm).

Phone Home

The teenage boy is such a difficult creature to knit for. But if you've knitted something for your daughter/niece/younger sister, then you can't leave out your son/nephew/younger brother… But what to make for a grouchy, slouchy teenage boy? Nothing pretty, no accessories…hmm. And then… Eureka!

This mobile phone cover is not too soppy a gift for a lad, and it has the additional use of protecting his mobile phone (or ipod) from getting battered in his school bag! Plus, it can be tailored to suit whichever sports team he supports (or if he's a grungy geek or a would-be rocker, try knitting it all in black and sewing on a pirate patch – yaar!). As a knitter, this project is a great way to use up oddments of yarn as it doesn't take much.

P.S. This is not just for the boys, I quite fancy a pink and purple one with sequins!

YOU WILL NEED

DOUBLE-KNIT YARN
any small amounts of double-knit you have will do

4MM KNITTING NEEDLES

DARNING NEEDLE

Handy HINT

In a pattern with so many colour changes, it is a good idea to keep a tally of the rows as you knit them so your stripes change accurately. And remember: colour changes must always sit at the same end of your knitting.

ABBREVIATIONS:

K = Knit

St(s) = Stitch(es)

START KNITTING

Cast on 25sts (in first color – red)

Knit 16 rows.

Cast off 6sts, Knit to end. Count 19sts.

Cast off 6sts, Knit to end. Count 13sts.

Change to second colour - white.

Knit 16 rows.

Change to first colour - red.

Knit 32 rows.

Change to second colour - white.

Knit 14 rows.

Change to first colour - red.

Knit 2 rows.

Turn so that the stitches are in your left hand and empty needle in right, cast on 6sts. Count 19sts.

Knit 1 row.

Turn so that the stitches are in your left hand and empty needle in right, cast on 6sts. Count 25sts.

Continuing in first colour – red, Knit 16 rows.

Cast off. Weave in all ends – make sure you weave the ends on the wrong side of the work (where the colour change is not as tidy).

1 Fold the piece in half inside out along the dotted line and sew up the sides, underarms, sleeves and shoulders, leaving a 3- or 4-cm gap at the 'neck' to insert the phone into. This gap should be a bit smaller than the width of the phone, so that it will stretch to put the phone in and the phone won't fall out. Then turn it right side out and pop the phone in.

Remember to use red yarn to sew up the red section and white yarn to sew up the white section (or whatever colours you've chosen).

2 I decorated the phone cover by cutting numbers and letters out of felt and sticking them on with fabric glue. Try using initials, numbers, or your favourite football player's team number.

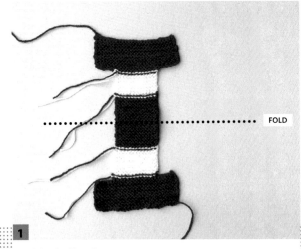

FOLD

1 Fold in half and sew up

2 Decorate your phone home with glued on felt pieces

Manly Scarf

This is a variation on the theme of the ordinary scarf. I've added a couple of twists to take it away from the image of the granny-knitted present and given it a direct route to modern-man-chic.

Garthenor Organic yarn and 7mm knitting needles used in this image

It is also fun for the knitter as it uses a 2x2 rib which, while it may take a bit longer to knit, makes for great practice in knitting and purling – and it incorporates a funky stripe as well. Choose your colours with care – is the man-in-mind an avid supporter (or loather) of a football team that sports particular colours? Does he have favourite colours, or colours he strictly avoids? A stripe can say so much about a man. Decisions, decisions…

YOU WILL NEED

200G CHUNKY-WEIGHT YARN
This will usually require a 7 or 8mm knitting needle). You need 100g each of two different, carefully chosen colours of yarn, to give 200g in total.

7/8MM KNITTING NEEDLES
(Look at the yarn label).

Handy HINT

K2, yf, P2, yb will create a 2x2 rib
The movements of the yarn are not
shown in the pattern, as the knitter
will know where the yarn needs to
be to keep the pattern and stitch
count even.

But as a beginner you should count
your stitches at the end of every row,
and if you forget where you are in the
middle of a row, go to the stitches that
you've already knitted (on the right
hand needle) and count what you've
already done: e.g.: "k2, p2, k2, p2…
what's next? Oh yes, k2. Is my yarn at
the back? It is? Keep working!"

ABBREVIATIONS:

K = Knit

P = Purl

St(s) = Stitch(es)

YF = Yarn forward

2x2 Rib = knit two stitches, purl two stitches

START KNITTING

Cast on 28sts

Knit 2 sts, Purl 2 sts. Repeat this sequence of k2, p2, to the end of the row.

Repeat this row for a total of 10 rows.

Change to next colour.

K2, P2, rib for 10 rows.

Change to next colour.

K2, P2, rib for 10 rows.

Continue this sequence until the scarf has eleven stripes in each colour.

Cast off in 2x2 rib.

1 **WEAVE IN ALL YOUR ENDS**
Weave your ends in vertically along the edge of the scarf.

1 Weave in your ends vertically on 2x2 rib

Handy HINT

Casting off in 2x2 rib
K1, K1, cast off 1. (Yarn forward. P1, cast off 1. P1, cast off 1. Yarn back. K1, cast off 1. K1, cast off 1). Repeat to end of the row remembering to knit and purl in the same places that you have been throughout the scarf.

Knitter's Notes

Rib Reminder: Remember that when you knit, the yarn is at the back of the work (furthest away from you) and when you purl, the yarn is at the front of the work (between the needles and your body).

Weaving the ends along the length of the scarf, rather than along the width, helps retain the elasticity of the rib stitch.

Girlie Scarf

A variation on a regular scarf, this is a floaty, feminine piece that is more of an adornment than a way to keep warm.

It is also more of a challenge, in that the yarn working for you in this scarf is a definite step up from the standard yarns we've been using so far.

The fact that this piece is so pretty means that all the ladies – from your four-year old princess to your grandmother – will be vying to wear it!

You'll be using a very fine mohair yarn; this looks more like thread than yarn, and feels utterly luxurious. Using needles far larger than recommended gives a faux lace effect and also knits up super quick. Although this yarn is challenging for a beginner knitter (it will be hard to see, let alone undo, mistakes), any little mistakes disappear in the beauty of the yarn and the loose weave.

This scarf works well on a mild spring day, or, as I mostly use it, in the evenings as more of a wrap. It is perfect to jazz up a simple outfit, and so quick to knit that you'll want to make one in every colour!

YOU WILL NEED

25G EXTRA FINE MOHAIR
(I love Colinette's hand painted 'Parisienne' or Rowan 'Kid Silk Haze')

8MM KNITTING NEEDLES

Knitter's Notes

With this pattern, you are using knitting needles several sizes bigger than recommended on the yarn label. This gives a very open weave to your work and creates a lacy effect that's very pretty, and satisfying for a beginner to knit.

Handy HINT

A few tricks to remember when knitting this scarf:
• Keep your stitches much looser than you usually would. It will make the knitting easier, and won't affect the pattern.

• If you add new yarn, tie an extra knot - weaving in ends won't be very secure in such an open weave.

• My guinea pigs have preferred bamboo needles as they are less slippery when knitting such loose stitches.

• And don't worry if it looks a bit odd in the beginning – this yarn may be more difficult to get used to working with, but it's very forgiving and hides all mistakes beautifully! Persevere.

ABBREVIATIONS:
St(s) = Stitch(es)

START KNITTING

Cast on 30 sts loosely

Knit every row until the scarf measures 100cm (or your desired length). This scarf works well in different lengths. Try casting off after 70cm or 150cm.

Cast off very loosely.

Give to your favourite lady (or keep it for yourself!) Original, simple and very beautiful...

Using fine yarn and bigger needles gives a faux lace effect

Little 'n' Large Cushions

You can easily knit all sorts of beautiful items for your home - a knitted cushion adds a lovely original touch to a chic, modern interior, or makes a cosy addition to a traditional room.

This versatile pattern is knitted using a 'basket weave' stitch pattern, and can be used to make a chunky cushion, or a smaller scented knit pillow to fragrance your linen closet. You use the same pattern, just different yarn, needles and filling depending on whether you are knitting the large or little size.

Using the same pattern you can make a scent pillow or a chunky cushion cover

Basket weave stitch

YOU WILL NEED

SMALL SCENTED CUSHION

50G DOUBLE-KNIT YARN
(any oddments of double-knit yarn will do nicely)

4MM KNITTING NEEDLES

THREE SMALL (1 CM) BUTTONS

DRIED LAVENDAR OR POT POURRI

AN OLD PAIR OF TIGHTS OR SOCKS

DARNING NEEDLE

LARGE CUSHION

200G SUPER BULKY YARN
(Rowan 'Big Wool' is perfect for the large cushion cover)

12MM KNITTING NEEDLES

THREE LARGE BUTTONS
– approx 4cm diameter

DARNING NEEDLE

CUSHION PAD
this should be around 5-10cm bigger than your finished cushion cover so that your knitting stretches tight over the pad. This will show off your basket weave to its best advantage.

PATTERN LAYOUT

Fold in half inside out at the fold lines, with the short ends of the piece in the middle.

KEY TO DIAGRAM

Fold lines
Button holes

START KNITTING

······································· FOLD LINE

······································· FOLD LINE

FINISH KNITTING

ABBREVIATIONS:

K = Knit

P = Purl

St(s) = Stitch(es)

YF = Yarn forward

K2tog = Knit two stitches together

START KNITTING

Cast on 24sts.

Row 1: (K4, P4), repeat to end of row.

Rows 2-5: Repeat this row a further four times.

Row 6: (P4, K4), repeat to end of row.

Row 7-10: Repeat this row a further four times.

Repeat this ten-row pattern a further five times.

You will count twelve squares running vertically on your piece of knitting, and six squares horizontally.

1 Buttonhole row: K4, yf, K2tog, K5,yf, K2tog, K5, yf, K2tog, K4.

K 1 row.

Cast off.

Weave in all ends.

2 Fold in half inside out at the fold lines, with the short ends of the piece in the middle.

3 Sew up the sides of the cushion cover, working from the centre towards the edge.

Turn right-side out. Sew on three buttons to correspond with buttonholes.

FINISHING

LARGE
Squeeze cushion pad into your knitted cover, and pull tight on the buttons to fasten them shut.

4 ### LITTLE
Cut the foot off an old pair of clean tights, fill it with potpourri or dried lavender and sew it firmly closed. Use this as a mini cushion pad to stuff into your little cover. This one doesn't need to be stuffed as tightly as the large cushion.

Handy HINT

To knit a basket weave practice square:

Cast on 24sts.

K4, P4, repeat to the end of the row.
Repeat the above row a further 3 times (4 in total).

P4, K4, repeat to the end of the row.
Repeat the above row a further 3 times (4 in total).

Repeat these 8 rows until you have knitted a practice square.

1 Three buttonholes

2 See fold lines on layout diagram

3 Sew up using backstitch

4 Fill scent pillow with potpourri or dried lavender

Enjoy and Experiment

One thing that you mustn't forget is that this learning-to-knit business is fun! Don't get stressed or frustrated. There will always be a more experienced knitter not very far away, who you can ask for help.

Patterns are just a starting point - you should use them as a guide rather than as a set of strict and inflexible rules. The best knitters bring their own style, ideas and creativity to each project they work on.

Mix and match the patterns you have been given in this book in any way you want to. Go wild in your colour choices. Try things even if you aren't sure they'll work. You never know what you'll discover (about knitting and yourself)!

Some ideas to start you off:

• Create the full Baby Combo: get your (or anybody else's) new addition kitted out in matching hat, mitts, cardigan and booties;

• Knit a His 'n' His Manly Scarf set, or Hers 'n' Hers Girly Scarves;

• Try knitted flowers on EVERYTHING!

• Embellishments: sew buttons, sequins, ribbons, patches, or anything else you fancy onto your knitting;

• Play with different-sized needles to create different effects and sizes: large needles = bigger item; small needles = smaller item.

Onwards and Upwards

So now, if you've been following the instructions in this book, you should be able to:

- cast on;
- cast off;
- knit;
- purl;
- increase;
- decrease;
- add stripes or embellishments to your work;
- create stitch patterns;
- sew up your knitting;
- follow a basic pattern; and
- make lots and lots of wonderful knitting!

What's next? Well, you may look at commercial knitting patterns and still feel confused. That's to be expected. At least now though you should be able to approach them knowing that you are knitting perfect stitches, you've got a few decent projects under your belt, and you feel confident in your ability to learn some new techniques.

Remember:

- Count your stitches every row.

- Don't abandon your work in the middle of a row – it's very easy to forget where you are.

- Remember to tick off your rows as you work them on the pattern so that you don't forget where you are.

- If you are unhappy with your work, don't be afraid to start again.

- There are loads of brilliant knitters around every corner…ask for help!

What's next for you to learn?

- Tension squares and their importance in creating fitted garments.

- Abbreviations – there are more out there that we haven't covered. Sl1, psso, kfb – don't worry, they'll all have translations.

- Techniques – for every method of doing something that you've learnt in this book, there are 5 more out there. You will encounter increasing by knitting into the stitch more than once, decreasing by passing stitches over, and endless methods of casting on. Find your own favourite techniques.

- Knitting patterns – there are millions to choose from. I suggest you start on patterns labelled for beginners; even in them you'll have lots of new exciting things to learn.

Good luck and happy knitting.

Useful Notes: Conversion Charts and Abbreviations

It would be much less confusing if everyone in the world could agree on just one system of measurement for sizes, lengths and weights, but we might be waiting a while for that to happen. So, until then, here are some useful facts and figures to help you with your knitting wherever in the world you may be.

Conversion Charts

KNITTING NEEDLE SIZES	
UK - mm	USA
2	0
2.5	1
2.75	2
3	2
3.25	3
3.50	4
3.75	5
4	6
4.5	7
5	8
5.5	9
6	10
6.5	10.5
8	11
10	15
12	17
15	19

CENTIMETRE - INCHES	
CENTIMETRE	INCHES
1	0.39
5	1.97
10	3.94
15	5.9
20	7.87
25	9.84
30	11.8

YARN WEIGHT	
GRAMS	OUNCES
25	0.88
50	1.76
75	2.65
100	3.5
150	5.29
200	7.05
250	8.81

YARN	
UK	USA
2 PLY	LACE WEIGHT
4 PLY	FINGERING
DOUBLE KNIT	SPORT/DOUBLE KNIT
ARAN	WORSTED
CHUNKY	BULKY

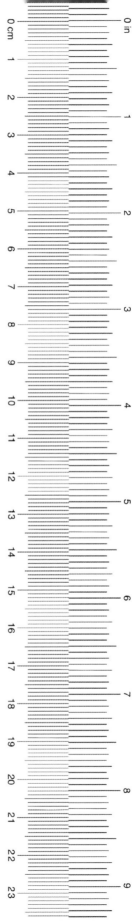

Abbreviations

Beginners often ask me why knitting patterns include such a lot of abbreviations. Well, the short answer is that, if they didn't, all the patterns would be pages and pages longer than they are! I've used as few abbreviations in my patterns as I can – I want all my patterns to be beginner-knitter-user-friendly above all else. But if I hadn't included some abbreviations (quite apart from the fact that this book would be 500 pages long!), you as a beginner wouldn't have had the chance to become accustomed to all the abbreviations you will undoubtedly come across in knitting patterns during your knitting career.

To help you, I have explained the abbreviations used in each pattern along the way, but here is a revision list of all the abbreviations used in the book.

K = Knit
P = Purl
St = Stitch
Sts = Stitches
St st = Stocking stitch
Dec = Decrease
Inc = Increase
Rep = Repeat
Tog = Together
K2tog = Knit two stitches together
M = Make a stitch: increase
YF = Yarn forward
YB = Yarn back
CF = Cable forward
CB = Cable back
DK = Double-knit yarn

Stockists

Colinette
www.colinette.com
Beautiful hand-painted luxury yarns

Debbie Bliss
www.debbieblissonline.co.uk
Gorgeous yarns, stylish patterns and more!

Garthenor Organic Yarns
www.organicpurewool.co.uk
Soil Association certified organic knitting yarns

Get Knitted
www.getknitted.com
Terrific shop and online store with some
hard-to-find yarns as well as all the favourites,
and knitting accessories

Hip Knits
www.hipknits.co.uk
Luxurious hand-painted yarns and fibres

I Knit London
www.iknit.org.uk
Shop, groups and sanctuary for knitters

John Lewis
www.johnlewis.com
Good selection of favourite yarns and accessories

Loop
www.loop.gb.com
London yarn boutique with knitting supplies sourced
from all over the world

Rowan
www.knitrowan.com
Yarns, patterns, knitting books, workshops and
much more

Sirdar
www.sirdar.co.uk
A great source for yarn and accessories – look out for
their amazing novelty yarn selection